MEMORABLE
EDINBURGH HOUSES

MEMORABLE EDINBURGH HOUSES

by
WILMOT HARRISON

With a new Introduction
by
J. B. BARCLAY

Republished S.R. Publishers Ltd., 1971
First published Edinburgh and London, 1893

ISBN 0 85409 731 7

Please address all enquiries to S.R. Publishers Ltd.
(address as above)

Reprinted by Scolar Press Ltd.,
Menston, Yorkshire, U.K.

Any bibliography for the city of Edinburgh must extend to many pages but there are some classics that are real works of reference and mines of information. Such a book is Wilmot Harrison's "Memorable Edinburgh Houses" which was revised and enlarged by Oliphant Smeaton as long ago as 1898. It has been unobtainable for nearly half a century but now comes back for the connoisseur historian of the city and the discerning visitor to it.

Harrison's book is, of course, limited in its compass. The Edinburgh of which he wrote was a much smaller place. Many houses in what to him were the suburbs were new and had not had enough time to become "memorable". He would not recognise the city today. From the turn of the century Edinburgh expanded rapidly. Portobello became part of the city in 1896 and so just manages to get into the book. By 1900 the boundary had extended to Duddingston, Restalrig and Granton. After the first world war Leith which had originally been controlled by Edinburgh returned after eighty-seven years of independence. The same period saw the parishes of Liberton, Colinton, Corstorphine and Cramond absorbed to create the greater Edinburgh of the twentieth century which stretches right to the summits of the nearer Pentland Hills. In this period estates were swallowed up in housing schemes, such as Niddrie, Craigmillar, Royston, Pennywell and Granton, while the occupants of the stately homes in the older city moved to Blackhall, Barnton, Craiglockhart, Colinton, Braids and beyond.

At the turn of the century railways crossed the city from many suburban stations but now even the lines have gone and there are only four passenger stations within the city boundary. Streets and houses were just beginning to be lit by gas or electricity. The motor car was a novelty on the streets where the cable-car was taking the place of the horse-bus. Such is the period of which Wilmot Harrison wrote.

The old Royal Mile had become a slum in 1900 but of late it has been largely reconstructed. People of substance have returned to live there. The stately homes of the New Town have been turned over to commercial interests. Office girls and clerks now carry tea and files where formerly butlers served the wine after dinner. Many streets mentioned in Harrison have changed their names and still more have disappeared entirely. For instance, Braid Place has become Sciennes House Place, Duncan's Land in the old Kirk Loan is now a largely derelict building of uncertain fate in Gloucester Lane. St James' Square has vanished for a new city centre group of buildings: Charles Street, General's Entry and the neighbourhood have been levelled for academic development: Lauriston Lane is lost in the Royal Infirmary and Brown Square and its companions have vanished from Chambers Street. Grange House with its curious architecture and legends is no more but other great houses have been preserved in modern scholastic establishments. Merchiston Castle, home of Napier of logarithm fame, is appropriately the central feature of the new Napier Technical College: Bruntsfield House and Ravelston House have each been incorporated in girls' schools. Craigcrook Castle is now an architect's office and Bonaly Tower is used by Boy Scouts.

The long list of Edinburgh celebrities of the last seventy years who would have appeared in a new edition of Harrison include many whose fame stretches far beyond the city boundaries. Charlotte Square would list the birthplace of Earl Haig who led the British forces in the first world war and did so much for the British Legion, Lord Lister of antiseptic surgery fame and the home of the Marquis of Bute which he has granted to the nation to be the official residence of H.M. Secretary of State for Scotland. Edinburgh now has its "grace and favour" residence at 36 Moray Place first occupied by the then Dean of the Thistle and Chapel Royal, Dr Charles L. Warr. Writers would mention Sir Compton Mackenzie and Moray M'Laren: artists would include Sir William MacTaggart and Sir Stanley Cursiter: architects of international repute would name Sir Basil Spence or Sir Robert Matthew.

Edinburgh houses remember discoverers or inventors like Alexander Graham Bell of telephone fame and J. Clerk-Maxwell whose wireless ray led to modern radar while among the principals of the University Sir Edward Appleton discovered the Appleton layer in the heavens and Sir Alfred Ewing was the genius of intelligence in the first world war who "cracked" the enemy codes. Norman Dott was a pioneer of brain surgery and Robert Philip of the treatment of tuberculosis. Masson, Saintsbury and Grierson adorned the English chairs in the University: R. K.

Hannay, Hume Brown and Richard Lodge those in history. There was a host of eminent judges, legal authorities and divines. Sir Donald Pollock gave of his wealth to the University for halls of residence: Sir Donald Tovey was the master of music whose programme notes have been used throughout the world: Sir Godfrey Thomson was the inspiration of the Moray House tests which were used worldwide to select pupils for post-primary schooling: and in the realm of song Sir Harry Lauder, born in Portobello, would find a place in a new Harrison as Scottish ambassador of the music hall stage.

So long as Edinburgh remains the capital of Scotland, the centre for the government departments in Scotland, the home of the General Assembly of the Church of Scotland, the location of the Supreme Courts of the country, the seat of the University, and the headquarters of most banks, insurance and investment companies, so long will Edinburgh have a succession of great inhabitants to occupy homes that will be remembered and the need will continue for the publication of more volumes of the Wilmot Harrison type to record the past and to make the ageing houses even more "memorable" still.

J. B. BARCLAY

MEMORABLE EDINBURGH HOUSES

MEMORABLE

EDINBURGH HOUSES

BY

WILMOT HARRISON

AUTHOR OF 'MEMORABLE LONDON HOUSES,' 'MEMORABLE
DUBLIN HOUSES,' ETC.

*With 38 original Illustrations from Drawings
made expressly for this work*

PUBLISHED BY

OLIPHANT ANDERSON AND FERRIER

30 ST. MARY STREET, EDINBURGH, AND

24 OLD BAILEY, LONDON

1893

PREFACE

THE success attending the production of the author's work on *Memorable London Houses*—two large editions having been nearly exhausted in six months—has induced the belief that a 'Handy Guide' to Edinburgh on a similar plan would meet with an appreciative reception. The purpose and scope of the book is to indicate the abodes of eminent persons in the past; and where 'improvements' have eradicated these, their former situation in those cases where the immediate vicinity is unchanged or but slightly altered; so that the surroundings of their former tenants retain at least sufficient characteristics of the past to feed the imagination of the visitor. Such biographical incidents and anecdotal illustrations of character and conduct are introduced as may lend additional interest to particular houses, or bring the personality of their former occupants the more vividly before the reader. The works of Chambers, Wilson, Grant, and others have of course been consulted; but the book is largely the result of independent inquiry and research, and many houses are indicated to which attention has not been directed in any work dealing with the subject.

W. H.

CONTENTS

ROUTE I

ROUTE II

ROUTE III

ROUTE IV

SUBURBAN ROUTES

ROUTE I.

THE OLD TOWN.

STARTING from the Esplanade of the Castle to descend

CASTLE HILL,

Ramsay Lodge is seen on the slope of the hill to the north—the best view is to be obtained from the approach from the New Town by the Mound—and, as it now appears, is an enlargement of the 'goose-pie' constructed by ALLAN RAMSAY the Poet as his domestic retreat from the cares of business. Daniel Wilson, in *Memorials of Edinburgh*,—says : 'Ramsay applied to the Crown for as much ground from the Castle Hill as would serve him to build a cage  for his *burd*, meaning his wife, to whom he was warmly attached, and hence the octagon shape it assumed, not unlike an old parrot-cage. If so, she did not live to share its comforts, her death having occurred in 1743. Here the poet retired in his sixtieth year.' Further, we learn that he was extremely proud of his new mansion, and appears to have been somewhat surprised that its fantastic shape rather excited the mirth than the admiration of his fellow-citizens. The wags of the town compared it to a goose-pie, and on his complaining of this one day to Lord Elibank, his lordship replied, 'Indeed, Allan, when I see you in it, I think they are not far wrong.' Ramsay died in 1758, at the age of seventy (see RAMSAY, p. 9).

ALLAN RAMSAY, portrait painter to the King and Queen, and son of the poet, enlarged the house on coming into possession of it on his father's death. The elder Ramsay writes

A

to an artist friend : 'My son Allan has been pursuing your science since he was a dozen years old; was with Mr. Halliday at London for some time about two years ago; has been since at home, painting here like a Raphael; sets out for the seat of the Beast beyond the Alps within a month hence, to be away two years.' The artist was a man of exceptionally attractive manner.   Allan Cunningham says : 'He led the life of an accomplished man of the world and public favourite' (*Lives of the Painters*), and Dr. Johnson said of him : 'You will not find a man in whose conversation there is more instruction and elegance than in Ramsay's.' Chambers refers in the *Traditions* to the romantic character of his marriage as apparently unknown to his biographers. 'In his early days, while teaching the art of drawing in the family of Sir Alexander Lindsay of Evelick, one of the young ladies fell in love with him; captivated, probably, by the tongue which afterwards gave him the intimacy of princes, and was undoubtedly a great source of success in life. . . . A marriage with consent of parents was impossible.   The young couple nevertheless contrived to get themselves united in wedlock.'   Ramsay settled in London, and died at the age of seventy-one in 1784.

The REV. DR. BAIRD, Principal of the University, lived, at a much later period, in Ramsay's house.   Anderson (*History of Edinburgh*) says : 'He was a man of kindly and benevolent disposition, and took an active part in the General Assembly's schemes for educating the inhabitants of the Highlands and Islands of Scotland.'   He lived 1761-1840.

On the left of Castle Hill is **James's Court.** The building facing the first entrance, and bearing the date 1690, stands on the site of a 'land'[1] that possesses a triple celebrity.   Its first memorable occupant was DAVID HUME.   Burton, in his *Life of Hume*, says : 'By ascending the western of the two stairs facing the entry of James Court, to the height of three stories, we arrive at the door of Hume's house, which, of the two doors on that landing, is the one towards the left.'   This was the residence of Hume from 1762, when he removed from Jack's Land.   After his absence in France he returned hither, and afterwards removed to the house he built for himself in St Andrew Square. 'Of the first impression made on a stranger at that period,'

[1] A term which the uninitiated reader may be informed is a synonym for the English word 'house' while the term 'house' is often applied to a flat or story.

says Burton, 'when entering such a house, a vivid description is given by Sir Walter Scott in *Guy Mannering*; and in counsellor Pleydell's library with its collection of books, and the prospect from the window, we have probably an accurate picture of the room in which Hume spent his studious hours when he was in his own house in Edinburgh.' Boswell writes: 'I always lived on good terms with Mr. Hume, though I have frankly told him I was not clear that it was right of me to keep company with him: "but," said I, "how much better you are than your books!" He was cheerful, obliging, and instructive. He was charitable to the poor, and many an agreeable hour I have passed with him.' Burton repeats an anecdote of him to the effect that having once given by a mistake a guinea to a beggar, the man, 'who was a respectable member of his trade,' returned it, and explained the mistake. He was permitted to keep the coin, the philosopher observing, 'O Honesty—how poor a dwelling-place hast thou found!' (see HUME, pp. 5, 19, 50.)

The REV. DR. HUGH BLAIR occupied Hume's house during his absence in France. Blair was at this time in the prime of life, and enjoying the reputation derived from the delivery of his *Lectures on Rhetoric and the Belles Lettres*. Later on he was astonished to find that, as a result of Dr. Johnson's good opinion of his first volume of sermons, a publisher was prepared to pay him £100 for it, and frankly expressed his astonishment to that gentleman. This was a foretaste only of the ultimate advantages, which included a pension from George III. of £200 as a result of some of the sermons having been read to him by the eloquent Lord Mansfield. The Editor of *Kay's Edinburgh Portraits* says that the worthy Doctor 'indulged to a considerable extent in light reading, *The Arabian Nights* and *Don Quixote* being among his especial favourites. ... He was vain, and very susceptible of flattery. His taste and accuracy in dress were absolutely ridiculous. ... He was so careful about his coat that, not content with merely looking at himself in the mirror to see how it fitted in general, he would cause the tailor to lay the looking-glass on the floor, and then, standing on tiptoe over it, he would peep athwart his shoulder to see how the skirts hung.' Having requested the artist who painted his portrait to depict him with 'a pleasing smile,' and assumed that expression at the artist's request, the literal representation proved to be so idiotic a grin that the picture was destroyed, and a second painted, in which no special effect was attempted. In *Kay's Portraits* the following anecdote is given: 'During the latter part of his life almost all strangers of distinction who visited Edinburgh brought letters of introduction to Dr. Blair. . . . On one of these occasions, when he had collected a considerable party at dinner to meet an English clergyman, a Scotchman present asked the stranger what was thought of the Doctor's sermons among his professional brethren in the south. To his horror, and to the mortification of Mrs. Blair who sat near, and who looked upon her husband as a sort of divinity, the Englishman answered, "Why, they are not partial to them at all." "How sir?" faltered out the querist, "how should that be?"—"Why," replied the southron, "because they are so much read, and so generally known, that our clergy can't borrow from them."' 'Blair was timid and unambitious,' writes Dr. Alexander Carlyle of Inveresk (*Autobiography*), 'and withheld himself from public business of every kind; and seemed to have no wish but to be admired as a preacher, particularly by the ladies. His conversation was so infantine that many people thought it impossible, at first sight, that he could be a man of sense or genius. He was as eager about a new paper to his wife's drawing-room, or his own new wig, as about a new tragedy or a new epic poem.' Blair died in 1800, aged sixty-two (see BLAIR, p. 116).

JAMES BOSWELL, the third noteworthy tenant of James's Court, was also an occupant of the third flat, having rented it of Hume, and here he received SAMUEL JOHNSON as his guest. 'On Saturday, the 14th of August 1773,' he writes, 'late in the evening I received a note from him that he was arrived at Boyd's inn, at the end of the Canongate. . . . I went to him directly. He embraced me cordially, and I exulted in the thought that I now had him actually in Caledonia. Mr. Scott's [his travelling companion] amiable manners, and attachment to the Socrates, at once united me to him. He told me that before I came in, the Doctor had unluckily had a bad specimen of Scottish cleanliness. He then drank no fermented liquors. He asked to have his lemonade made sweeter; upon which the waiter, with his greasy fingers, lifted a lump of sugar and put it into it. The Doctor in indignation threw it out of the window. Scott said he was afraid he would have knocked the waiter, down. Mr. Johnson and I walked arm in arm up the High Street. . . . It was a dusky night: I could not prevent his being assailed by the evening effluvia of Edinburgh.' Burton, Hume's biographer, suggests that the 'arch-intolerant' would probably not have been able to 'sleep o' nights' if he had known that the previous tenant of the rooms in which he had been enjoying Boswell's hospitality was the man who, as is reasonably conjectured, was the subject of the remark at Mrs. Piozzi's 'that he had the *lumières*,' and of Johnson's rejoinder; 'just enough to light him to hell.' It is related that Boswell, while showing his hero about, met Henry Erskine in the Potterrow, and introduced him to his friend. Erskine having heard of the kind of reputation the good Doctor had acquired since his arrival in the city, returned his bow with nothing more than 'Your servant, sir,' and passed on, taking care, however, to slip a shilling into Boswell's hand, 'for the sight of the *bear* with which he had been favoured.'

At the foot of Castle Hill is the

LAWNMARKET.

Riddle's Close is on the right on south side. Entering, we find a projecting turret-stair belonging to the land which has its front windows on the street. This was the first residence of DAVID HUME as an independent householder in Edinburgh. He removed hither from Ninewells in 1751, and here he produced his *Political Discourses*, and, from a comparison of dates, little doubt can exist that he commenced his *History of England* here, though it was written, for the greater part, in Jack's Land. Writing of his removal here, Hume says: 'I have now at last—being turned of forty . . . arrived

RIDDLE'S COURT.

at the dignity of being a householder. About seven months ago I got a house of my own, and completed a regular family, consisting of a head, viz. myself, and two inferior members—a maid and a cat. My sister has since joined me, and keeps me company' (Burton's *Life of Hume*).

The building facing the visitor on passing through the second large archway, accounted 'a fair sample of the houses of the better sort at the end of the sixteenth century,' and reported to have received King James VI. as a guest, is identified, as regards the first floor above the street, with the worthy Bailie and rich merchant, JOHN MACMORAN, who had the honour to play the host to royalty, and the misfortune to come by his death from a pistol-shot fired by a schoolboy, on going with a posse to force the door of the High School. The pupils, being discontented in respect of their holidays, having barred themselves up, and, being duly provisioned, refused to surrender until their demands were complied with. The aristocratic connections of the young homicide served to protect him from the punishment of his rash and foolish, if not criminal, escapade.

Recrossing the Lawnmarket we enter

Lady Stair's Close.—Here is 'a substantial old mansion presenting, in a sculptured stone over the doorway, a small coat-armorial with the initials " W. G." and "G. S.", the date 1622, and the legend "Fear the Lord and depart from evil." The letters refer to Sir William Gray of Pittendrum, the original proprietor of the house, and his wife' (Chambers's *Traditions*). Here, on the second flat of a common stair, lived ELIZABETH, DOWAGER COUNTESS OF STAIR, the leader of Edinburgh Society in the early part of last century, and the first to keep a black domestic servant. Her matrimonial adventures: how she had to leap half-dressed from an open window to escape the savage brutality of her first husband, Viscount Penrose; how a fortune-teller subsequently showed her, in a 'magic mirror,' her absent lord about to marry another woman, and the prevention of the ceremony by her own brother—events which were afterwards found to have occurred at the precise time of the vision; how on Lord Penrose's death Lord Stair contrived to compel her to break her vow of remaining single by gaining admission to her house and exhibiting himself at a prominent window *en déshabille* to the possible injury of her reputation; how he knocked her down after marriage in a drunken fit, and repentantly agreed when sober to drink no more in future than she permitted,—are to be found recorded in the *Traditions of Edinburgh*, and will be recognised by readers of Scott as the foundation of his story *My Aunt Margaret's Mirror*. Lady Stair died in 1759. The date of her birth is uncertain.

In this Close lived 'Honest JOHN PATON,' who contrived, on eighty pounds a year, as clerk in the Custom House, to live until eighty-seven years of age, and accumulate a collection of books, manuscripts, coins, etc., which it took nearly six weeks to sell by auction: who, if the account of his mode of life be strictly accurate, took no food until four in the afternoon, when a cup of coffee and a slice of bread served him till the nine o'clock supper at John Downie's tavern— 'a bottle of ale, and a gude buffed herring or roasted skate and ingans.' A vision of his 'neat plain dress and black wig' haunts us as we quit the court, and 'the sound of his cane upon the pavement as he descended'—his signal always for admittance—seems to ring in our ears.

Baxter's Close.—Here ROBERT BURNS lodged in the first stair to the left and on the first floor, an apartment of fair dimensions. 'Having  met with Professor Dugald Stewart, then one of the leading celebrities of Edinburgh, Burns was induced to set out on a visit to the Scottish capital, where he arrived on the 28th of November of the same year [1786] and shared with an acquaintance, John Richmond, a writer's clerk, a humble lodging in Baxter's Close, Lawnmarket, of which the weekly rent was three shillings sterling' (Anderson's *Scottish Nation*). 'The tradition of his residence,'

BAXTER'S CLOSE.

says Wilson, 'has passed through very few hands; the predecessor of the present tenant . . . . learned it from Mrs. Carfrae [the landlady], and the poet's room is pointed out, with the window looking into Lady Stair's Close' (*Memorials of Edinburgh*). Lockhart (*Life of Burns*) says: 'During the winter Burns continued to lodge with John Richmond, and we have the authority of this early friend of the poet for the statement that while he did so "he kept good hours." He removed afterwards to the house of Mr. Nicoll (one of the teachers of the High School of Edinburgh), on the Buccleuch Road; and this change is, I suppose, to be considered a symptom that the keeping of good hours was beginning to be irksome. . . . With a warm heart the man united a fierce, irascible temper, a scorn of many of the decencies of life, a noisy contempt of religion, at least of the religious institutions of his country, and a violent propensity for the bottle.' In April 1787 Burns wrote to Dr. Moore: 'I leave Edinburgh in the course of ten days, or a fortnight. I shall return to my rural shades, in all likelihood never again to quit them. I have formed many intimacies and friendships here, but I am afraid they are all of too tender a construction to bear carriage of a hundred and fifty miles.' Cockburn, in his *Life of Jeffrey*, describes him, on one occasion, when a boy of thirteen, as standing in the High Street staring at a man whose appearance struck him as remarkable; when a person tapped him on the shoulder, and said, 'Ay, laddie, you may weel look at that man!—that's Robert Burns.' Scott says of the poet: 'His person was strong and robust, his manner rustic, not clownish, a sort of dignified plainness and simplicity. . . . I think his countenance was more massive than it looks in any of his portraits. There was a strong expression of sense and shrewdness in all his lineaments; the eye alone, I think, indicated the poet's character and temperament. It was large, and of a cast which glowed, I say literally *glowed*, when he spoke, with feeling or interest. His conversation expressed perfect self-confidence, without the slightest presumption. . . . I have only to add that his dress corresponded with his manner. He was like a farmer, dressed in his best to dine with the laird' (Lockhart's *Life of Scott*). Burns died in 1796, at the age of thirty-seven (see BURNS, p. 70).

We now pass into the

HIGH STREET.

Passing the Exchange on the left, and St. Giles's Church on the right we reach, on the left, by Cockburn Street, **Miln's Square.** In a part of the large building on the west side, the EARL OF HOPETOUN (Sir James Hope) whose equestrian statue stands in front of the Royal Bank in St. Andrew Square, held vice-regal state. The writer of the obituary notice in the *Annual Register* of 1823, says: 'As the friend and companion of Moore and as acting under Wellington in the Pyrenean campaign, he had rendered himself conspicuous. But it was when, by a succession to the earldom, he became the head of one of the most ancient houses in Scotland, and the possessor of one of its most extensive properties, that his character shone in its full lustre. . . . An open and magnificent hospitality, suited to his place and rank, without extravagance or idle parade, a full and public tribute to the obligations of religion and private morality without ostentation or authority . . . a kind and generous concern in the welfare of the humblest of his dependants—

these qualities made him beloved and respected to an extreme degree, and will cause him to be long remembered.' He died 1823, at the age of fifty-seven.

Below North Bridge, on the left, giving itself 'bold advertisement,' stand the remains of the House of ALLAN RAMSAY.

ALLAN RAMSAY'S HOUSE.

The two upper stories were removed about forty years since. Here, 'at the sign of the Mercury' the author of the *Gentle Shepherd* lived and laboured as author, printer, editor, and publisher; issuing his poems singly in sheets or half-sheets, in which shape they had a ready sale. They were sold at a penny, and the worthy citizens would send their children with the coin for 'Allan Ramsay's last piece.' In 1725 he removed from here to the Luckenbooths, since abolished; nearly all his original publications were issued at the 'Mercury' (see RAMSAY, p. 1).

Dickson's Close is nearly opposite to Ramsay's house. On entering the close, the first house on the left was, in 1788, the residence of DAVID ALLAN, 'the Scottish Hogarth.' Here he took aristocratic pupils at a guinea per month for three lessons in the week, while fulfilling his functions as Master of the Academy established by the Board of Trustees for Manufactures and Improvements. In the year above-named he published an edition of the *Gentle Shepherd*, with characteristic drawings. From Brown's edition of that work we extract the following description of the artist, of whom it may be premised that he came prematurely into the world, and had the misfortune in early infancy to be dropped out of a basket into the road, severely cutting his head, while being conveyed a long distance to a nurse whose capabilities for affording him the requisite nourishment were of the exceptional nature required by the extreme smallness of his mouth. 'He was under the middle size; of a slender feeble make, with a long, sharp, lean, white, coarse face much pitted by the smallpox, and fair hair. His large, prominent eyes, of a light colour, were weak, near-sighted, and not very animated. His nose was long and high, his mouth wide, and both ill-shaped. His whole exterior to strangers appeared unengaging, trifling, and mean; and his deportment was timid and obsequious. The prejudice naturally excited by these disadvantages at introduction was, however, dispelled on acquaintance, and as he became easy and pleased, gradually yielded to agreeable sensations. . . . When in company he esteemed, and which suited his taste, as restraint wore off, his eyes imperceptibly became active, bright, and penetrating; his manner of address quick, lively, and interesting,—always kind, polite, and respectful; his conversation open and gay, humorous without satire, and playfully replete with benevolence, observation, and anecdote.' He died in 1796, at the age of fifty-two.

No. **58** High Street, at the head of South Gray's Close, bearing a memorial tablet—an example which might be followed

elsewhere with advantage —was the residence of Henry David, tenth Earl of Buchan. Here HENRY ERSKINE and his younger brother THOMAS, afterwards LORD CHANCELLOR ERSKINE, were born in 1746 and 1749 respectively. 'The present tenants,' writes Colonel Fergusson, the biographer of Henry Erskine, in 1872, 'of the Erskine mansion have a tradition of its former greatness, and of the *débris* of the title-deeds of a former tenant — a certain Lady Mary Hamilton — having been found under the remains of an ancient marble hearthstone.' The fortunes

HEAD OF GRAY'S CLOSE.

of the Buchan family are described as having been far from flourishing, and comfort was maintained only by a careful economy. 'Lady Buchan had a housekeeper who regulated all out-goings very rigidly, and called forth the indignation of the boys by often telling them, when some dainty dish was set upon the table, "Noo, boys, ye're no to tak ony o' yon : I've just sent it up for the lo'e o' my lord." This frugality on the part of the old housekeeper was probably the cause of the following effusion from the pen of Thomas Erskine ; the first specimen extant of those *Thread-paper Rhymes* for which the Lord Chancellor enjoyed a certain reputation :

> ' " Pa is going to London,
>   And what will be got then, oh !
> But sautless kail, and the old cow's tail,
>   And half the leg of a hen, oh !" '

The mansion of the Earl of Stirling, known also as ' Argyll's Lodging '—having passed to the family of Argyll about 1640 —in South Gray's Close, and having its entrance in Hyndford Close, has disappeared along with the latter locality, redolent formerly of memories of Dr. Rutherford, uncle of Scott, and of the poet's boyhood ; of Lady Anne Lindsay, author of *Auld Robin Gray*, and of Lady Maxwell, whose daughter, after-wards to become the famous Duchess of Gordon, was once encountered mounted on a sow of which she had made capture, when despatched to fetch a ' kettle ' of water from the ' Fountain Well in front of John Knox's house,' while her sister, Miss Betty, afterwards Lady Wallace, 'thumped it with a stick '—as recorded in Fergusson's *Life of Henry Erskine.*

' **John Knox's House,**' unquestionably the most ' memor-able ' of Old Town houses, was considered by Chambers (*Traditions of Edinburgh*) to be ' perhaps the oldest stone building of a private nature now existing here : for it was in-habited, before Knox's time, by George Durie, Abbot of Dun-fermline, promoted to Dunferm-line by James V. in 1539.' Knox occupied it during his incum-bency as minister of Edinburgh from 1560 till his death, receiv-ing £200 a year Scots money and living rent-free. His first wife died soon after, and here he brought his second spouse, whose affections his defamers affirmed he gained by sorcery.

JOHN KNOX'S HOUSE.

Chambers (*Traditions of*

Edinburgh) infers 'from the size of the house and the variety of accesses to it,' that Knox occupied only a portion of it, and that this was probably the first floor. From the window in the angle of the building containing his effigy, the great Reformer is said, by tradition, to have addressed the people beneath. M'Crie (*Life of Knox*) tells how in 1571, when he was obnoxious to the adherents of Queen Mary, 'one evening a musket-ball was fired in at his window, and lodged in the roof of the apartment in which he was sitting. It happened that he was sitting at the time in a different part of the room from that which he had been accustomed to occupy, otherwise the ball, from the direction it took, must have struck him.' In confirmation of the view that Knox occupied the first floor, Chambers remarks that 'the second floor is too high to have admitted of a musket being fired in at one of the windows. A ball fired in at the ground floor would not have struck the ceiling.' It was here that the great Reformer received the messengers of Queen Mary, the nobles of the court, and the leaders of the Congregation. Over nearly the whole front extends a long inscription, but concealed in great part by sign-boards. The word 'as' in brackets is obliterated: LVFE GOD ABOVE AL AND YOVR NICHTBOVR [AS] YI SELF. Dr. M'Crie, in his *Life of Knox*, thus refers to his physical characteristics: 'There are perhaps few who have attended to the active and laborious exertions of Knox, who have not been led insensibly to form the opinion that he was of a robust constitution. This is, however, a mistake. He was of small stature, and of a weakly habit of body; a circumstance which serves to give a higher idea of the vigour of his mind. His portrait seems to have been taken more than once during his life, and has been frequently engraved. It continues still to frown in the bed-chamber of Queen Mary, to whom he was often an ungracious visitor. We discern in it the traits of his characteristic intrepidity, austerity, and keen penetration. Nor can we overlook his beard, which, according to the customs of the time, he wore long, and reaching to his middle; a circumstance which I mention rather because some writers have assured us that it was the chief thing which procured him reverence among his countrymen. A popish author has informed us that he was gratified at having his picture drawn, and expresses much horror at this, after he had caused all the images of the saints to be broken.' He lived 1505-1572.

Tweeddale Court is reached by a passage nearly opposite

to Knox's house. The mansion of the MARQUESS OF TWEED-DALE is at the foot of the close, now in the occupation of Messrs. Oliver and Boyd, publishers. Wilson (*Memorials*) says it is 'mentioned by Defoe among the princely buildings of Edinburgh, "with a plantation of lime-trees behind it, the place not allowing room for a large garden " . . . latterly its gardens extended to the Cowgate. Successive generations of the Tweeddale family have occupied the house till the general desertion of Edinburgh by the nobility soon after the union.' The fourth Marquess was Secretary of State for Scotland : a predecessor, described as 'perhaps as good a specimen as could be selected of the weathercock politicians of uncertain times,' was High Chancellor of Scotland under William III. He died here.

It is stated in Wilson's *Memorials* (1868) that 'the question remains as interesting as ever " Who murdered Begbie?"' Doubtless, in these bustling days, the question has less interest; but mention may be made in passing, that, according to Wilson, the mysterious murderer of the ill-fated bank-porter in 1806 probably pounced upon his victim from within the entry to a stair on the right hand side of the close on entering.

High Street now merges into the

CANONGATE.

Morocco Land, No. 275 Canongate, an antique gabled façade with stone basement, and a curious figure of a tur-baned Moor occupying a pulpit projecting from a recess over the second floor, derives its name and interest from the legend which assigns its occupancy to ANDREW GRAY, who escaped the gallows as a leader of a riotous attack on the Provost's house, to become the prisoner of pirates, a slave, and ultimately in favour with the Emperor of Morocco, to lay the city of Edinburgh under contribution as a pirate in his turn, and finding the Provost of the time to be a relation of his own, cured his daughter of the plague, married her, and settled down as a peaceable citizen. Having vowed, however, never to enter the city but sword in hand, he kept the vow till his death, having never again passed the threshold of the Nether Bow Port.

Turning out of the Canongate on the left is

NEW STREET.

At the first house in the right, standing on the rear of
No. 247 Canongate, formerly 'the self-contained house at the
head of New Street fronting the Canongate on the east
side,' presumably with a garden in front—a house then considered one of the first in the city—lived HENRY HOME,
LORD KAMES, who became a judge of the Court of Session in
1752. His biographer, Tytler, says of him: 'Lord Kames
was in his person extremely tall, and of a thin and slender
make. In his latter years he had a considerable stoop in his
gait; but when in the vigour of life, and particularly when
in his dress as a barrister, his appearance is said to have
been uncommonly becoming. His countenance, although
not handsome, was animated.' 'He possessed the dangerous
and powerful engine of sarcasm,' says a writer in Chambers's
Biographical Dictionary, 'but he used it to heal, not to
wound. The following instance of his reluctance to give
pain, to be found in a letter to Mr. Creech, is so characteristic
of a truly worthy man that we cannot abstain from quoting
it. "In the fifth volume of Dodsley's collection of poems,
there is one by T—— D—— at page 226, which will make a
good illustration of a new rule of criticism that is to go into
a new edition of the *Elements*; but as it is unfavourable to
the author of that poem, I wish to know whether he is alive;
for I would not willingly give pain.' Tytler says that in
every period of life he 'was fond of social intercourse; and
with all his ardour of study and variety of literary and professional occupation, a considerable portion of his time was
devoted to the enjoyments of society.' The following anecdote is from the same source: 'Mrs. Home, who had a taste
for everything that is elegant, was passionately fond of old
china; and, soon after the marriage, had made such frequent
purchases that way as to impress her husband with some little
apprehension of her extravagance. But how to cure her of
this propensity was the question. After some consideration
he devised an ingenious expedient. He framed a will, be-
queathing to his spouse the whole china that should be found
in his possession at his death; and this deed he immediately
put into her hands. The success of the plot was complete:
the lady was cured from that moment of her passion for old
china.' This story illustrates the statement in *Kay's Edinburgh Portraits* that 'notwithstanding the general gravity
of his pursuits, his lordship was naturally of a playful dis-

position and fond of a harmless practical joke.' 'Not more than four days before his demise,' says the same writer, 'a friend called on his lordship, and found him, although in a state of great languor and debility, dictating to an amanuensis. He expressed his surprise at seeing him so actively employed. "Would ye have me stay with my tongue in my cheek till death comes to fetch me?" A day or two after this he told the celebrated Dr. Cullen that he earnestly wished to be away, because he was exceedingly curious to learn the nature and manners of another world. He added, "Doctor, as I never could be idle in this world, I shall willingly perform any task that may be imposed on me in the next."' Lord Kames died in 1782, at the age of eighty-six.

The house at the lower corner of the first lane on the left is of interest as the residence of LORD HAILES (SIR DAVID DALRYMPLE), who died here in 1792. He was elevated to the bench in 1766. Robert Chambers, in *Traditions of Edinburgh*, says: 'When Lord Hailes died, it was a long time before any will could be found. The heir-male was about to take possession of the estate to the exclusion of his eldest daughter. Some months after his lordship's death, when it was thought that all further search was vain, Miss Dalrymple prepared to retire from New Hailes, and also from the mansion in New Street, and while a maidservant was closing the window shutters Lord Hailes's will dropped out upon the floor from behind a panel, and was found to secure her in the possesion of his estates," which she enjoyed for upwards of forty years.' Paterson, however, in *Kay's Edinburgh Portraits*, says that this account is incorrect. 'The conveyance was found, not by a female servant while cleaning out the house in New Street, but by persons properly authorised on the first or second day after the funeral. It was carefully wrapt up in one of the drawers of a small chest in his lordship's dressing-room.' The library described as the 'fine room which held his books' was shown to Robert Chambers in 1825. It still contained them. He was also told that Lord Hailes 'wrote most of his works by the parlour fireside, where sat his wife and children.' 'His constitution, of which he was careful, as well as his principles and habits, rendered him averse to every kind of dissipation. After he was constituted a judge he considered it unbecoming his character to mingle much with the fashionable and gay world. He is described as affectionate to his family and relations, simple and mild in his manners, pure in his morals, enlightened and entertaining in his conversation.'

(Chambers's *Biographical Dictionary*).　Lord Hailes was born in 1726, and died at the age of sixty-six.

Nearly opposite New Street in the Canongate is

ST. JOHN STREET.

The house at the head of the street, and facing the Canongate, No. 22, was the residence of the Earl of Hope-

toun at one period; but has acquired a more interesting celebrity as the abode of TOBIAS SMOLLETT during his second visit to Edinburgh in 1766, with his sister, Mrs. Telfer, who occupied the first floor. Smollett was in an infirm state of health, but mixed occasionally in the best society of the town. Dr. Alexander Carlyle, who was very intimate with him and introduced him to several persons, whose characteristics afterwards amused the readers of *Humphry Clinker*, says of him: 'Smollett was a man of very agreeable conversation, and much

SMOLLETT'S HOUSE.

genuine humour; and, though not a profound scholar, possessed a philosophical mind, and was capable of making the soundest observations on human life, and of discerning the excellence or recognising the ridiculousness of every character he met with' (*Autobiography*). Mrs. Telfer 'is described,' writes Chambers, 'as a somewhat stern-looking specimen of her sex, with a high cast of features; but in reality a good-enough-natured woman; and extremely shrewd and intelligent. One passion of her genus possessed her—whist. A relative tells me that one of the city magistrates, who was a tallow-chandler, calling upon her one evening, she said, "Come, bailie, and take a trick at the cartes." "Troth, ma'am," said he, "I have ne'er a bawbee in my pouch." "Tut man, ne'er mind that," replied the lady; "let's e'en play for a pund o' candles!"' (*Traditions of Edinburgh*).

At No. **10**, in the second decade of the century, lived
JAMES BALLANTYNE. In Lockhart's *Life of Scott* we read:
'James Ballantyne then [1818]
lived in St. John Street, a row
of good old-fashioned and
spacious houses, adjoining the
Canongate and Holyrood, and
at no great distance from his
printing establishment. . . . I
have occasionally met the poet
in St. John Street when there
were no other guests but Erskine, Terry, George Hogarth,
and another intimate friend
or two; and when James
Ballantyne was contented to
appear in his own true and best
colours, the kind head of the
family, the respectful but
honest schoolfellow of Scott,

10 ST. JOHN STREET.

the cosy landlord of a plain comfortable table. But when any
great event was about to take place in the business, especially
on the eve of a new novel, there were doings of a higher strain
in St. John Street, and to be present at one of these scenes
was truly a rich treat even—if not especially—for persons
who, like myself, had no more knowledge than the rest of
the world as to the authorship of *Waverley.* There were
congregated about the printer all his own literary allies, of
whom a considerable number were by no means personally
familiar with the GREAT UNKNOWN—who, by the way, owed
to him that widely adopted title :—and *he* appeared among
the rest with his usual open aspect of buoyant good humour,
although it was not difficult to trace in the occasional play
of his features the diversion it afforded him to watch all
the procedure of his swelling confidant, and the curious
neophytes that surrounded the well spread board.' Lockhart's estimate and opinion of Ballantyne respecting the
financial difficulties of Sir Walter Scott seem in no way
based on his eminent father-in-law's opinion ; for Scott writes :
'I have been far from suffering from James Ballantyne. I
owe it to him to say that his difficulties as well as his advantages are owing to me.' It is said that Scott originated pro-
jects which proved unprofitable for the interest of the
publishing firm, and that they were carried out in opposition
to Ballantyne's judgment. 'Na, na, Mr. Scott, you are clean
wrong,' said the Ettrick Shepherd to Scott on one occasion,

in a conversation reported in Hogg's *Domestic Manners and Private Life of Scott*, 'for Johnnie Ballantyne tauld me, an' he could na but ken.' 'Ay, but ye should hae ascertained whether it was leeing Johnnie or true Johnnie who told you that before you avouched it; for they are two as different persons as exist on the face of the earth. Had James told you so, you might have averred it, for James never diverges from the right forward truth.' 'James,' says Hogg, 'was a man of pomp and circumstance, but he had a good affectionate heart. It was too good and too kind for this world; and the loss, first of his lady, and then of his great patron and friend, broke it; and he followed him instantly to the land of forgetfulness.' Lockhart described James Ballantyne as 'a short, stout, well-made man, and would have been considered a handsome one, but for those grotesque frowns, starts, and twistings of his features, set off by a certain mock majesty of walk and gesture, which he had, perhaps, contracted from his usual companions, the emperors and tyrants of the stage. His voice in talk was grave and sonorous, and he sang well (theatrically well) in a fine rich bass.' Ballantyne was born 1772, died 1833 (see BALLANTYNE, pp. 91, 98).

At No. 13 lived JAMES BURNETT, LORD MONBODDO, of whom Cockburn wrote that his peculiarities were 'classical learning, good conversation, excellent suppers, and ingenious though unsound metaphysics.' 'The admiration of classic literature,' says the editor of *Kay's Edinburgh Portraits*, 'led Lord Monboddo to get up suppers in imitation of the ancients. These he called his *learned* suppers. He gave them once a week, and his guests were Drs. Black, Hutton, and Hope.' Anticipating Darwin, he asserted in his work on the *Origin and Progress of Language* that the human race were originally endowed with tails; and in Chambers's *Traditions of Edinburgh*, we read: 'So convinced is he said to have been of the truth of his fantastical theory of human tails, that whenever a child happened to be born in his house, he would watch at the chamber door, in order to see it in its first state; having a notion that the midwives pinched off the infants' tails.' It was in allusion to this extraordinary discovery that Lord Kames, to whom he would on a certain occasion have given precedency, declined it by saying: 'By no means, my lord, you must walk first that I may see your tail.' He first arrived in Edinburgh on the forenoon of the day which terminated with the public murder of Captain Porteous; and it is said that when about to retire to rest, the tumult in the street attracted him to the door, half-undressed. He got entangled in the crowd of passers-by, and hurried along to the Grassmarket, where he was a witness to the last act of the tragedy. Conceiving this to be the normal condition of things in the city, as he lay sleepless through the night, he seriously contemplated leaving Edinburgh forthwith, as a place unfit for a civilised being to live in. 'Almost every year he visited London,' writes R. P. Gillies, 'performing, of course, the whole journey on horseback. . . . King George III. happening to inquire of his lordship, and of a military man successively, how they had come to town, found reason to remark on the answers: "Very odd, very odd! my judges gallop to town on horseback, and my cavalry officers travel snugly in the mail-coach"' (*Reminiscences of a Literary Veteran*). Riding was his sole means of locomotion; his objections to the use of a carriage being two-fold. First, that it was not consistent with the dignity of human nature to be dragged at the tails of horses; and second, that the ancients did not commonly use such effeminate conveyances. 'The manners of Lord Monboddo,' says Chambers (*Traditions*), were not more odd than his person. He looked rather like an old stuffed monkey draped in a judge's robe, than anything else. His face, however, bore traces of high intellect.' Dean Ramsay, in his *Reminiscences of Scottish Life and Character*, remarks that 'he was a very powerful man, and could walk fifty miles a day; his usual refreshment on the road being a bottle of port wine, poured into a bowl, and drunk off at a draught.' We conclude our notice of this singular man with a second extract from Lord Cockburn's *Memorials*: 'Some offence made him resolve never to sit on the same bench with President Dundas; and he kept this vow so steadily that he always sat at the Clerk's table, even after Dundas was gone. . . . It is more common to hear anecdotes about his maintaining that men once had tails, and similar follies, than about his agreeable conversation and undoubted learning. All who knew him in Edinburgh concur in describing his house as one of the most pleasant in the place. Burns was a frequent guest here. He commemorates the early death of Miss Burnett in one of his poems. Monboddo died in 1799, at the advanced age of eighty-five.

CANONGATE.

No. **229,** the house on the north side, opposite to St. John Street, stands on the site of **Jack's Land**. It was to one of the flats here that DAVID HUME removed from Riddle's Close, and here he finished his *History of England*. In 1762 he removed to James's Court. Lockhart's description of Hume's portrait

in *Peter's Letters* may fitly find a place here. 'The face is far
from being in any respect a classical one. The forehead is
chiefly remarkable for its prominence from the ear, and not
so much for its height. . . . His eyes are singularly prominent, which, according to the Gallic system, would indicate an extraordinary development of the organ of language
between them. His nose is too low between the eyes, and
not well or boldly formed in any other respect. The lips,
though not handsome, have in their fleshy and massive outlines abundant marks of habitual reflection and intellectual
occupation. The whole has a fine expression of intellect,
dignity, candour, and serenity.' Dr. Alexander Carlyle, in
his *Autobiography*, says: 'At this period, when he first
lived in Edinburgh, and was writing his *History of England*,
his circumstances were narrow, and he accepted the offer of
librarian to the Faculty of Advocates. [This brought him
£40 yearly: subsequently he gave the salary away. See
BLACKLOCK, p. 31.] . . . His economy was strict, as he loved
independency; and yet he was able at that time to give
suppers to his friends in his small lodgings in the Canongate.' Hume, Adam Smith, Adam Ferguson, Lord Elibank,
and Drs. Blair and Jardine would meet occasionally at a
tavern to sup together. 'I remember one night,' says Dr.
Carlyle, 'that David Hume, having dined abroad, came
rather late to us, and directly pulled a large key out of his
pocket, which he laid on the table. This, he said, was given
him by his maid Peggy (much more like a man than a
woman), that she might not sit up for him, for she said when
the honest fellows came in from the country he never returned till after one o'clock.' The other members of the
supper party were resident outside the town. Hume lived
1711-1776 (see HUME, pp. 25, 50).

LADY EGLINTOUN was a tenant of Jack's Land during her
latter years, a lady whose peculiar grace of manner gave
rise to the phrase 'Eglintoun air,' which continued in use
long after her death. Extremely tall, with a superb figure,
and features and complexion of remarkable loveliness, she
remained a widow after the death of her husband in 1729—
being then forty-two years of age. Her union with the Earl,
who was much her senior, was said to have been predicted
by her relatives and nurses from the circumstance of a
hawk with his lordship's name on the bells having alighted
on her shoulder while she was walking in her father's
garden at Culzean. It is also reported of her that the beauty
of her complexion, which she preserved to the last, was due

to the avoidance of the use of paint, and periodical bathing
with sows' milk. When Dr. Johnson visited her at Auchans,
he received an embrace and a kiss from her at parting, of
which he was afterwards very proud. Boswell says of her:
'Lady Eglintoun, though she was now in her eighty-fifth
year, and had lived in the country almost half a century,
was still a very agreeable woman. Her figure was majestic,
her manners high-bred, her reading extensive, and her conversation elegant.' Taming rats was the eccentric amuse-
ment of her latter years. She had a panel in the oak wain-
scot of her dining-room, which she tapped upon and opened
at meal-times, when a dozen rats came forth and partook
of her meal with her. She died in 1780, at the age of ninety-
three. When living in Jack's Land, she had no less than
seven daughters resident with her, all beautiful women, and
all, with one exception, fortunate in their marriage. A
striking picture is drawn in Fergusson's *Life of Henry
Erskine* of 'a procession of eight sedan chairs, each with
its couple of liveried bearers, carrying a lady in full ball
costume of feathers, sacque, etc., on their way to the
Assembly Rooms . . . in broad daylight. Great is the excitement as the procession emerges from Lady Eglintoun's
house in the Canongate, threads its way up the crowded
High Street till it reaches the Assembly Rooms.' And, later
on, 'when these fair ladies returned from the ball, with the
addition of flaming torches, and to each chair a gentleman
in attendance, drawn sword in hand, and hat obsequiously
in the other, according to custom, who guard the party till
they descend at their house in the aristocratic neighbourhood
of Jack's Land. As this goodly caravan winds its way down
the slopes of the Canongate, with wealth of cackle and
silvery laughter over the incidents of the ball, what fitter
subject for a last century picture than such a combination
of sedans, torches, swords, cocked-hats, and full-dressed
wigs; with flashes from bright eyes more deadly than from
swords; while from under the outside stairs the aroused
swine stare forth and wonder.'

A little below St. John Street stands, conspicuous with
its stone balcony, **Moray House,** until 1835 part of the
entailed estates of the house of Moray, in whose possession
it remained exactly two hundred years. 'It presents,' as we
read in Wilson's *Memorials of Edinburgh*, 'more striking
architectural features than any other private building in
Edinburgh, and is associated with some of the most interesting events of Scottish history.' It was built by Mary,

Countess of Home, in 1618, in the reign of Charles I.   In
1648 OLIVER CROMWELL 'took up his residence at "the
Lady Home's lodging in
the Canongate," as it then
continued to be called.'
According to Guthrie, he
communicated to the noble
leaders of the extreme
party of the Covenanters
'his design in reference to
the King, and had their
assent thereto,' in consequence of which 'the Lady
Home's house in the Can-
ongate became an object
of mysterious curiosity
from the general report at
the time that the design
to execute Charles I. was
there discussed and ap-
proved.' Two years after
Cromwell's visit, the fes-

MORAY HOUSE.

tivities attending the marriage of the unfortunate Earl of
Argyll, then Lord Lorne, with Lady Mary Stuart, eldest
daughter of the Earl of Moray, took place here; and the
wedding guests, with the bride and bridegroom, passed
out on to the old stone over-hanging balcony to gaze on
their old prostrate enemy, the Marquis of Montrose, as
he passed in a low cart, bound, and preceded by the hang-
man with a band of meaner prisoners, to his doom, and
'shrank back discomfited before the calm gaze of the cap-
tive.'   Wilson remarks : 'This remarkable incident acquires
a deeper interest, when we consider that three of these
onlookers, including the gay and happy bridegroom, perished
by the hand of the executioner on the same fatal spot to
which the gallent Marquis was passing under their gaze.'

The ancient building with a three-gabled front, below
Moray House, and bearing four Latin inscriptions, a transla-
tion of which, with other particulars, the non-classical visitor
may purchase for a penny at the stationer's shop now
occupying part of the premises, is identified with the families
of Huntly and Gordon, and dates from the middle of the
seventeenth century.

Panmure Close formerly led to Panmure House at the
end of the close ; the residence for many years of DR. ADAM

SMITH, author of *The Wealth of Nations*. The house was removed in the middle of the year 1889.

Whiteford House stands back from the end of Galloway's Entry, opposite the school built on the site of Milton House. Here, from about 1806 to 1812, lived DUGALD STEWART. 'There was, and perhaps is,' wrote R. P. Gillies in his *Reminiscences of a Literary Veteran*, in 1851, 'an old mansion in the regions of the Canongate, called Whiteford House, so commodious that it could be conveniently divided into two family residences, each complete in itself: one was the abode of Lord Bannatyne, the other of Dugald Stewart. It stood comparatively retired from the noise of the street, on a large ground, more than an acre, I think, shut in by walls and gateways. Within this enclosure there were some tall old trees. . . . His library was to the rear, and its windows looked to the grey rocks of Calton Hill.' Stewart, says Lord Cockburn, 'was about the middle size, weakly limbed, and with an appearance of feebleness which gave an air of delicacy to his gait and structure. His forehead was large and bald, his eyebrows bushy, his eyes grey and intelligent, and capable of conveying any emotion, from indignation to pity, from serene sense to hearty humour, in which they were powerfully aided by the lips, which, though rather large perhaps, were flexible and expressive. The voice was singularly pleasing; and, as he managed it, a slight burr only made its tones softer. . . . His gesture was simple and elegant, though not free from a tinge of professional formality; and his whole manner that of an academical gentleman.' (*Memorials of My Time*). In another place we read of 'an unimpeachable personal character, devotion to the science he taught, an exquisite taste, an imagination imbued with poetry and oratory, liberality of opinion, and the loftiest morality.' In his *Life of Jeffrey*, Cockburn quotes Mackintosh, who said that 'the peculiar glory of Stewart's eloquence consisted in its having breathed the love of virtue into whole generations of pupils.' He was troubled with a slight asthmatic tendency, which made it often necessary to clear his throat. When told of a remark that 'there was eloquence in his very spitting,' he said, 'I am glad, at least that there is one thing in which I had no competitor.' Stewart died in 1828, aged seventy-five (see STEWART, p. 84).

SIR WILLIAM MACLEOD, LORD BANNATYNE, who lived here till his death, is described by Wilson as 'a remarkably pleasing specimen of a gentleman of old Edinburgh, before its antique mansions and manners had altogether fallen under the ban of modern fashion. . . . He was raised to the bench on the death of Lord Swinton, and took his seat as Lord Bannatyne in 1799. He was the last survivor of the Mirror Club, and one of the contributors to that early periodical. His conversational powers were great, and his lively reminiscences of the eminent men and the leading events of last century are referred to by those who have enjoyed his cheerful society, when in his ninetieth year, as peculiarly vivid and characteristic' (*Memorials of Edinburgh*).

Queensberry Lodge, a large gloomy building enclosed in a court, and now used as a Refuge for the Destitute, was the town mansion of the DUKES OF QUEENSBERRY, and was built by William, the first Duke (died 1695), 'who exercised almost absolute power in Scotland during the latter years of the reign of Charles II.; and presided as High Commissioner in the first part of the reign of James VII., and afterwards took an active share in the revolution that placed the Prince of Orange on the throne. . . . A great miser, yet magnificent in buildings and pleasure grounds; illiterate, yet a collector of books; and commanding in his letters—which he dictated to a secretary—a style that is admirable' (Wilson's *Memorials of Edinburgh*). From the same source we learn that his son, the SECOND DUKE, 'the active promoter of the Union, and the Lord High Chancellor under whose auspices it was accomplished, kept court here during that stormy period; and frequently found his huge mansion was surrounded by the infuriated mobs who so pertinaciously pursued every abettor of that hated measure.' Chambers (*Traditions of Edinburgh*) relates a 'tale of mystery and horror,' preserved by tradition, about the eldest son of the second Duke, 'an idiot of the most unhappy sort—rabid and gluttonous, and who early grew to an immense height,' and was kept confined in an apartment on the ground floor of the western wing. Being on one occasion left alone in the house with a little kitchen boy who turned the spit, and free from the customary restraint, he found his way to the kitchen, killed the lad, and placed his body where the meat had been before the fire, half roasted it, and was found devouring it on the return of the family.' CHARLES, the THIRD DUKE, was born here; and here his Duchess, LADY KATHERINE HYDE, the famous beauty of the court of George I., whom Horace Walpole celebrated in her old age as 'Prior's Kitty ever fair,' and whose sprightliness and wit have been commemorated by Prior, Pope, and Swift, entertained the poet GAY, who stayed for some time here as a guest; 'Duchess Katherine,' writes Chambers, was 'eccentric to a degree bordering upon madness. . . . It is an undoubted fact that, before her marriage, she had been confined in a *strait jacket* on account of mental derangement, and her conduct in married life was such as to entitle her to a repetition of the same treatment. . . . Her Grace was no admirer of Scottish manners. One of their habits she particularly detested—the custom of eating off the end of a knife. When people dined with her at Drumlanrig, and began to lift their food in this manner, she used to scream out, and beseech them not to cut their throats; and then she would confound the offending persons by sending them a silver spoon or fork on a salver. . . . When in Scotland she always dressed herself in the garb of a peasant girl. Her object seems to have been to ridicule and put out of countenance the stately dresses and demeanour of the Scottish gentlewomen who visited her' (*Traditions of Edinburgh*). The successor to 'the Good Duke' was the Earl of March, the sporting character and debauchee, who became known as 'Old Q.,' and who caused Queensberry House to be stripped of its ornaments and sold in 1801. Chambers states that, 'with 58 fire-rooms, and a gallery seventy feet long, besides a garden, it was offered at the surprisingly low upset price of £900. The Government purchased it for a barrack.'

Whitehorse Close.—Here are the remains of the Whitehorse Inn, so-called, a tradition reported, according to Chambers, after a white palfrey belonging to Queen Mary. Wilson (*Memorials of Edinburgh*) puts its age at that of the date cut over a dormer window on the south front—1623, and says: 'The interest is much more legitimate which associates it with the Cavaliers of Prince Charles's court, as the quarters of Captain Waverley during the brief sojourn in the capital. It forms the main feature in a small paved quadrangle. . . . A broad flight of steps leads up to the building, diverging to the right and left from the first landing, and giving access to two singularly picturesque timber porches which overhang the lower story, and form the most prominent features in the view. A steep and narrow alley passes through below one of these, and leads to the north front of the building.' This building must not be confounded with Boyd's Whitehorse Inn, at which DR. JOHNSON lodged, and the site of which is commemorated by a tablet at the corner of St. Mary Street and Boyd's Entry.

ROUTE II.

THE OLD TOWN—(*Continued*).

OUR starting-point is the western extremity of the Cowgate, and is reached from the western end of the New Town by King's Stables Road, at the back of the Castle, and the Grassmarket; or from the middle of Princes Street by the Mound, Bank Street, and Melbourne Place, leaving the latter at Victoria Street.

COWGATE.

At the juncture of the Cowgate and Candlemaker Row is a tall stone land, interestingly associated with the events preceding the birth of LORD BROUGHAM in 1778. In some guide-books it is incorrectly stated that he was born here, and that he pointed out the window of the room (on the third floor) to Sir Robert Peel on one occasion. What he really did, doubtless, was to indicate the window of one of the rooms occupied by his parents at the time of their marriage, his birth having taken place, as expressly stated in his autobiography, at Lord Buchan's house in St. Andrew Square. Chambers (*Traditions of Edinburgh*) says: 'The Edinburgh tradition on the subject was that Henry Brougham of Brougham Hall in Cumberland, in consequence of a disappointment in love [his intended bride died on the eve of the day appointed for the wedding] came to Edinburgh for the diversion of his mind. Principal Robertson, to whom he bore a letter of introduction, recommended the young man to the care of his sister, Mrs. Syme, widow of the minister of Alloa.' Indicating the third floor as the residence of Mrs. Syme, the writer proceeds: 'It would appear Mr. Brougham speedily consoled himself by falling in love with Eleonora, the daughter of Mrs. Syme; and a marriage, probably a hurried one, soon united the young pair' (see BROUGHAM, p. 50).

Here also, above or below Mrs. Syme's floor, lived HENRY MACKENZIE, with his father Dr. Mackenzie. Mrs. Blacklock told Dr. Johnson (on an occasion when he consumed nineteen cups of tea at her table) that 'although Dr. Mackenzie had a large family, and was married to a lady who was his son's stepmother, nevertheless the son lived with his own wife and family in the same house, and the greatest harmony obtained among all the parties.' Mackenzie was probably living here when *The Man of Feeling* was written in 1771, and later, during his editorship of *The Mirror* and *The Lounger* in 1778 and 1785. He was born in 1745, and died 1831 (see MACKENZIE, p. 91).

At the southern end of Candlemaker Row, Bristo Street leads to

LOTHIAN STREET.

At No. **42** one of the flats was the residence of THOMAS DE QUINCEY. H. A. Page (*Life and Writings of De Quincey*) says: '42 Lothian Street was an address very familiar to De Quincey's friends or to curious persons for a long series of years. . . . The Lothian Street life ran alongside the Mavis Bush life in a very unique way.' 'My first lodging in Edinburgh,' writes R. Rowe (*Episodes of an Obscure Life*), 'were the rooms in Lothian Street in which De Quincey died. I was, in fact, their next tenant. The good people of the house, a widow, her maiden sister, and a niece, had a very worshipful recollection of their "nice little gentleman"— that was their phrase for him. They evidently liked

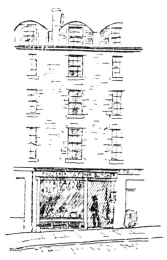

LOTHIAN STREET.

him, and said that he was "bonnie and soft spoken." . . . This maiden sister seems to have been really a mature guardian angel to De Quincey. More than once she said she had "put him out," when he had fallen asleep with his head on the table, and overturned a candle on his papers. She used to buy his apparel for him piecemeal; now a pair of socks, now a pair of boots, now a coat, now a waistcoat— never a whole suit.' 'I am somewhat weary of Lothian Street,' De Quincey wrote to his daughter, 'but should

Lothian Street spitefully retort that she is weary of me, *that* happens to be impossible, as I can prove, for she has never seen me. At the end of the penultimate (not the ultimate) week of May 1856, did I, the underwritten, enter upon these Wilsonian rooms or room; out of which stirred have I not in any street or streetlet, once only excepted, three or four weeks back, when I went to the theatre for the purpose of seeing and hearing Grisi.' In a letter of February 1855 is an indication of more healthful habits than those above described: 'I am in deadly depression of nervousness, spite of which, however, I meditate great exertions; and (with the benefit of a daily nine or ten miles' excursion) I believe I could accomplish my plans.' T. J. Hogg, quoted by Page, describes De Quincey as 'a noticeably small figure, attired in a capacious garment which was made too large, and which served the purpose of both under and overcoat. . . . It was some time before the extreme refinement of his face was noticed—not, indeed, till the voice, gentle, clear, and silvery, began to be heard, when the eye ceased to be diverted by a certain oddity in the general appearance and was attracted by the brow, which, from its prominence, gave an aspect of almost child-like smallness to the under face, and by the eyes, which, combined with a singular power of quiet scrutiny, suggested something of weariness.' The latest period of De Quincey's addiction to opium in large quantities, drinking it, as Thomas Hood said, as another would drink claret, was in the period 1841-44, at which latter date the physical suffering, which was the original cause of his resorting to it, seems to have greatly abated. He died at Lasswade, whither he had removed, 1859, having, in spite of the extraordinary trials to which his constitution had been subjected, attained the age of seventy-three.

At No. 11 'CHARLES DARWIN and his brother Erasmus took lodgings in October 1833, at Mrs. Mackay's house, four flights of steps from the ground floor.' This information was given by Mr. Francis Darwin to the writer of an article in the *Edinburgh Dispatch* for May 22, 1888. The Darwins were then attending the medical classes at the University.

South College Street, at the end of Lothian Street, leads into Nicolson Street, a short distance southward in which is

NICOLSON SQUARE.

At No. 3 was living in 1804-1816, DR. J. BORTHWICK GILCHRIST, the eminent Oriental scholar, who, though trained for the medical profession, in the exercise of which he went out to India, earned his degree as LL.D. by the remarkable lingual acquirements which gave an impetus to the study of Hindostanee among the servants of the East India Company previously unknown. His health compelled him to return home in 1804. Of his peculiar character an interesting account is furnished in Chambers's *Biographical Dictionary of Eminent Scotsmen*: 'On returning home, Dr. Gilchrist set up his residence in his native Edinburgh, and there his fiery Eastern temper, his liberal opinions in politics, which trenched upon republicanism, and his eccentricity of conduct, as well as of opinion, astonished the gravity of his wondering fellow-citizens. Being too impatient to be idle, he instituted, in conjunction with Mr. James Inglis, a bank in the Scottish capital . . . but the other banks, doubtful of its management, looked so unfavourably upon it, that the establishment after some time was closed. He set up an aviary at his house on the north side of Nicolson Square, the building being largely trellised with wire-work, and stored with all manner of bright and curious birds ; and the natives, who gazed and marvelled, thought it the strangest of Noah's arks, or the best of raree shows. From his strong language, especially at civic meetings, and his aptitude to take offence, he was liable to be involved in serious quarrels. . . . Such was Dr. Gilchrist in Edinburgh, and where these singularities were perhaps more vividly remembered in later periods than his talents, his kindliness and benevolence, by which they were more than counterpoised.' In 1816 he settled in London, where he derived a good income from tuition in Hindostanee and Persian. 'At this time his bushy head and whiskers were as white as Himalayan snow, and in such contrast to the active expressive face which beamed from the centre of the mass, that he was likened to a royal Bengal tiger—a resemblance of which he was proud.' He died in Paris in 1841, having reached the age of eighty-two.

NICOLSON STREET.

No. **58,** the Asylum for the Blind, was the residence of DR. JOSEPH BLACK, 'the illustrious Nestor,' as he was called by Lavoisier, 'of the chemical revolution,' whose discovery of latent heat may, it has been remarked, be said, through James Watt, who studied it, to have laid the foundation of the practical use of steam. As successor to Dr. Cullen in the Chair of Chemistry in Edinburgh in 1766, he rendered chemistry a fashionable study in Edinburgh, and it came to

be considered an essential part of the education of a gentleman. He is said to have been unambitious of distinction,
and of an indolent temperament, of delicate health, frugal
and methodical, but hospitable to the extent permitted by
his physical infirmities. Among his associates were Smith,
Hume, Carlyle, Home, and Hutton. Cockburn (*Memorials*)
says of him : ' He was a striking and beautiful person ; tall,
very thin, and cadaverously pale ; his hair carefully powdered,
though there was very little of it, except what was collected
into a long thin queue ; his eyes dark, clear, and large, like
deep pools of pure water. He wore black speckless clothes,
silk stockings, silver braces, and either a slim green umbrella,
or a genteel brown cane. The general frame and air were
feeble and slender. The wildest boy respected Black. No
lad could be irreverent towards a man so pale, so gentle, so
elegant, so illustrious. . . . He died seated, with a bowl of
milk on his knee, of which his ceasing to live did not spill a
drop ; a departure which it seemed after the event happened
might have been foretold of this philosophical gentleman.'
Cockburn gives also an amusing picture of Black and his
relative Sir Adam Ferguson—the two philosophers—' rioting
over a boiled turnip.' Black never married. His fortune was
disposed of in a most singular fashion, being ' divided into
one hundred shares, and parcelled out to a numerous list of
relatives in numbers or fractions of shares, according to the
degree in which they were proper objects of his care or
solicitude (Chambers's *Biographical Dictionary*). He died
in 1799 at the age of seventy-one. The building, which formerly had two windows on either side of the raised entrance,
was purchased for the Asylum in 1807.

At No. **94** the REV. THOMAS M'CRIE was living prior to
1821. We have given him the title which he himself preferred,
though possessing the degree of Doctor of Divinity. The
biography of John Knox, a work undertaken at a time ' when
he had the weekly and daily toil of a Scottish Secession
minister to interrupt him, as well as its very scanty emolu-
ments, to impede his efforts, and limit his literary resources,'
was published in 1811, and, highly praised by both the
Edinburgh and the *Quarterly Review*, at once achieved a wide-
spread success. But the production of this and other works,
and the intensity with which he entered into the ecclesiastical
controversies of the time, combined with the loss of his wife
in 1821, so affected his health, while his sight was so much
impaired with long examination of the dim and difficult
manuscripts which formed a large part of his biographical

researches, that he spent a long time abroad, and in 1822 settled, on his return, in Salisbury Place. Lockhart, in *Peter's Letters*, describes him as 'a tall slender man, with a pale face, full of shrewdness, and a pair of piercing black eyes—a shade of deep-secluded melancholy passing ever and anon across their surface, dimming their brilliancy. His voice, too, had a mild but very unpleasant shrillness in it sometimes.' Born in 1772, he died in 1835.

WEST NICOLSON STREET.

In a house at the west end of West Nicolson Street, looking towards St. Cuthbert's Chapel of Ease burying-ground, THOMAS BLACKLOCK, the blind poet, occupied the two upper flats on coming to Edinburgh in 1764. He had, however, been resident in Edinburgh ten years before, when his poems were first published, and when, after his leaving the city, Hume wrote to Matthew Sharp of Hoddam : 'I have enclosed this letter under one to my friend Mr. Blacklock, who has retired to Dumfries, and proposes to reside there for a time'; and requests him to 'send for a cargo' of the poems which Blacklock had just published by subscription, and many of which he pronounces to be 'extremely beautiful,' and 'to engage your acquaintance to purchase them.' Burton, Hume's biographer, says that Hume 'busied himself with many schemes for enabling his unfortunate friend to gain a subsistence, which might make him enjoy "the glorious privilege of being independent," but with small success.' He presented Blacklock with his salary as librarian of the Advocates' Library for two or three years, during which he retained the office—for his own convenience of having access to the books—while under censure from the committee for introducing certain French works on his own responsibility. Blacklock's settlement here in 1764 was subsequent to his rejection by the parishioners of Kirkcudbright as a pastor on account of his infirmity, and the adjudication of a moderate annuity as compensation. His ministerial career thus cut short, he resorted to receiving boarders into his house, some of whom also conducted their studies under his supervision. It was in consequence of the letter which Blacklock wrote to Burns on the first appearance of his poems that Burns relinquished his emigration scheme and came to Edinburgh, where Blacklock introduced him to many friends. This was in 1786. Dr. Johnson was entertained here at tea by Mrs. Blacklock in 1773. Blacklock is described as a man of most amiable disposition and gentle manners, warm to intensity in his feelings, and witty and entertaining in his conversation. He was fond of music and carried a flageolet in his pocket, the use of which he said had been suggested to him in a dream. A curious story of somnambulism is told in the memoir prefixed to his works in Anderson's *British Poets*, as having occurred at an inn at Kirkcudbright on the day of his ordination, when Blacklock, having fallen asleep after dinner, 'was called on by a friend, answered his salutation, rose and went with him into the dining-room, where some of his companions were met. He joined with two of them in a concert, singing as usual, with taste and elegance, without missing a note or forgetting a word. He then went to supper and drank a glass or two of wine. His friends, however, observed him to be a little absent and inattentive; by and by he began to speak to himself, but in so slow and so confused a manner as to be unintelligible. At last, being pretty forcibly roused, he awoke with a sudden start, unconscious of all that had happened, as till then he had continued fast asleep.' Blacklock died in 1791, at seventy years of age.

Windmill Street, at the end of West Nicolson Street, and Windmill Lane, going south, lead into

BUCCLEUCH PLACE.

No. **18** possesses a strong literary interest. FRANCIS JEFFREY brought his newly married wife here in 1801. ' A bold step,' writes Brougham, in his own *Life*, 'for his father was unable to assist him; his wife (Miss Catherine Wilson) had no fortune; and his professional income did not exceed £100 a year. They took a house,—or, to speak more correctly, a third floor or a flat in Buccleuch Place,'—' Not in either the eighth or ninth story, neither of which ever existed, but in the third story of what is now No. 18.' This reference of Cockburn's (*Life of Jeffrey*) is to Sydney Smith, who, probably prompted by a humorous impulse to indicate the enormous elevation of many Edinburgh houses, wrote of the first discussion of the *Edinburgh Review* as follows : ' Towards the end of my residence in Edinburgh, Brougham, Jeffrey, and myself happened to meet in an eighth or ninth story or flat in Buccleuch Place. I proposed that we should set up a review; this was received with acclamation. I was appointed editor, and remained long enough in Edinburgh to edit the first number. The motto I proposed was "*Tenui musam meditamur avena*"—" We cultivate literature on a little oatmeal." This was too near the truth to be admitted.

. . . When I left, the *Review* fell into the stronger hands of Jeffrey and Brougham, and reached the highest point of popularity and success' (*Preface to Collected Writings of Sydney Smith*). On this statement, Brougham remarks : 'Nothing can be more imaginative than nearly the whole account. In the first place, there never was a house eight or nine stories high in Buccleuch Place, or in any of that portion of the New Town of Edinburgh. No house at that time exceeded three stories. In the second place, Smith was never appointed editor.' He admits, however, that he superintended the production of the first number. Later on, Brougham writes : ' I can never forget Buccleuch Place, for it was there, one stormy night in March, 1802,

13 BUCCLEUCH PLACE.

that Sydney Smith first announced to me his idea of establishing a critical periodical, a review of works of literature and science. I believe he had already mentioned this to Jeffrey and Horner; but on that night the project was for the first time discussed by Smith, Jeffrey, and me.' Jeffrey removed from here to Queen Street (see JEFFREY, pp. 42, 55, 63, 84, 105).

A short passage at the west end of Buccleuch Place leads into

GEORGE SQUARE.

At No. **25** resided, at the close of the last century, Mr. Walter Scott, Writer to the Signet, described by Lockhart as 'a most just, honourable, and conscientious man, who, as a relative is reported to have said of him, "passed from the cradle to the grave without making an enemy or losing a friend."' Here the youth and young manhood of SIR WALTER SCOTT were passed, and so far was his father from having any prescience of his celebrity that he once said of him in reply to young Walter's expression of a taste for wandering, flute in hand, like Goldsmith over Europe, 'I greatly doubt, sir, you were born for nae better than a gangrel scrape-gut.' As

C

a reminiscence of his school-days Scott in the general preface to the Waverley Novels, tells of the conflicts with the boys

25 GEORGE SQUARE.

of the Crosscauseway, Bristo Street. and the Potterrow, who sometimes carried the battle into the precincts of the square. Being attacked by a swelling in his ankle—the cause of his subsequent lameness — a prolonged confinement to the house first led to his love of reading and the acquisition of a large store of knowledge. Then, when, an apprentice to his father, the time came for his law-studies, he tells, in the fragment of autobiography prefacing Lockhart's *Life* how 'a little parlour was assigned to me in my father's house, which was spacious and convenient; and I took the exclusive possession of my new realms with all the feelings of novelty and liberty. Let me do justice to the only years of my life in which I applied to learning with stern, steady, and undeviating industry.' Narrating how, while studying with his friend William Clerk for mutual benefit, he found the arrangement for alternate early morning meetings at each other's houses fall through on account of his friend's resolution being 'inadequate to severing him from his couch,' he 'agreed to go every morning to his house, which being at the extremity of Princes Street, New Town, was a walk of two miles—with great punctuality, however, I beat him up to his task every morning before seven o'clock.' In the concluding paragraph of his brief autobiographic fragment, he says: 'My father and mother, already advanced in life, saw little society at home, except that of near relations, or upon particular occasions; so that I was left to form connections in a great measure for myself.'

Jeffrey, calling on the young student, found him 'in a small den in the sunk floor of his father's house surrounded with books.' The following description by Lockhart of the 'den' was obtained by him 'from a lady of Scott's family.' 'Walter had soon begun to collect out-of-the-way things of all sorts. He had more books than shelves; a small painted cabinet with Scotch and Roman coins in it, and so forth; a claymore, a Lochaber axe given him by old Invernahyle, mounted guard on a little print of Prince Charlie; and *Broughton's Saucer* was hooked up against the wall below it. Such was the germ of the magnificent library and museum at Abbotsford . . . . Since those days the habits of life in Edinburgh as elsewhere have undergone many changes, and the "convenient parlour" in which Scott first showed Jeffrey his collections of minstrelsy is now, in all probability, thought hardly good enough for a menial's sleeping room.' In Wilson's *Memorials of Edinburgh* (1869) it is stated that the room 'possesses one valuable memento—on one of the window panes his name is still seen, inscribed with a diamond in a school-boy hand.' From George Square, when at College, Scott used to make excursions in the vacation, in company with John Irving and 'three or four books from the circulating library,' to Salisbury Crags, Arthur's Seat, or Blackford Hill, and there feast together—both from the same book and Scott the most quickly — on Spenser, Ariosto, Boiardo, and *The Castle of Otranto*. A rupture of a blood-vessel in the lower bowels laid him up for many weeks, when 'with his bed piled with a constant succession of works of imagination' he played eagerly at chess with Irving, not having then discovered, as in after life, that it was 'a sad waste of brains.' A slovenliness of attire which had previously characterised him seems to have been thrown aside in 1790, when a lady who remembered him well at the old Assembly Rooms told Lockhart he was 'a comely creature'; and he said of himself: 'It was a proud night with me when I first found that a pretty young woman could think it worth her while to sit and talk with me hour after hour, in a corner of the ball-room, while all the world were capering in our view.'

In the previous paragraph reference has been made to *Broughton's Saucer*. This was a relic which the young Walter had carefully preserved of a scene which took place here between the father and mother (a lady 'short of stature and by no means comely') of the poet. The lady's curiosity being excited by the mysterious passage from a sedan chair 'at a certain hour every evening' of a 'person carefully muffled up in a mantle' into the house, who was immediately ushered into her husband's private room, Mrs. Scott came, on one occasion, uninvited into the room just as the mysterious visitor was about to leave—on the pretence of bringing a cup of tea, as their interveiw had been so prolonged. When the stranger, 'a person of distinguished appearence and richly draped,' had received a cup, disposed of its contents, and withdrawn, Mr. Scott threw the empty cup out of the window; and, in reply to the lady's exclamation at the loss of her china, said: 'I can forgive your little curiosity, madam, but you must pay the penalty. I may admit into my house on a piece of business persons wholly unworthy to be treated as guests by my wife. Neither lip of me nor of mine comes after Mr. Murray of Broughton.' Murray was the traitorous secretary of Prince Charles Stuart (see SCOTT, pp. 56, 58, 66, 74, 75).

No. 24 or 26—which, is now unknown—was the residence of HENRY ERSKINE very shortly after the completion of the square, then considered the most fashionable part of Edinburgh. Fergusson (*Life of Erskine*) quotes the late Earl of Buchan [son of Henry Erskine] with reference to this period of his father's life: 'Walter Scott's family lived next them in the square, No. 25, and they met on friendly terms, though the difference of politics discouraged intimacy. I find the name of Walter Scott, W.S., frequently among my father's law-papers, and receipts for the rent of Scott's stables, which Henry Erskine took for his black horses. [His yellow carriage and black horses were a familiar sight in Edinburgh at this time.] Little Watty, before he could speak plainly, was always running in and out of our house, to my mother's great annoyance. She used to call him "that silly, tiresome boy."' Cockburn, in his *Life of Jeffrey*, says of Henry Erskine: 'His name can no sooner be mentioned than it suggests ideas of wit, with which, in many memories, the recollection is chiefly associated. A tall and rather slender figure, a face sparkling with vivacity, a clear, sweet voice, and a general suffusion of elegance, gave him a striking and pleasing appearance.' Brougham (*Life*) says: 'Harry Erskine both in society and in public was the most popular advocate —indeed the most popular man. His education was entirely confined to Edinburgh, but he had none of the accent or other provincialisms of the place. His taste was well cultivated, but far from severe. . . . His speaking was of a very high order.' The editor of *Kay's Edinburgh Portraits* describes him as 'above the middle size, and eminently handsome. His voice was powerful, his manner of delivery peculiarly graceful, his enunciation accurate and distinct.' The stories of Erskine's wit are innumerable, and many of them have been assigned to other eminent men. In *Kay's Portraits* we read in reference to his appointment as Lord Advocate during the coalition administration, in succession to Henry Dundas—afterwards Lord Melville: ' On the morning of the appointment he had an interview with Dundas in the Outer House, when, observing that the latter gentleman had already resumed the ordinary stuff gown which advocates are in the custom of wearing, he said gaily, that he "must leave of talking to go and order his silk gown" (the official costume of Lord Advocate and Solicitor-General). "It is hardly worth while," said Mr. Dundas, drily; "for the time you will want it you had better borrow mine." Erskine's reply was exceedingly happy: "From the readiness with which you make the offer, Mr. Dundas, I have no doubt that the gown is a gown made to *fit any party*; but, however short my time in office may be, it shall ne'er be said of Henry Erskine that he put on the *abandoned habits of his predecessors*." The predictions of Mr. Dundas proved true, however, for Erskine held office only for a very short period, in consequence of a sudden change of Ministry. He was succeeded by Ilay Campbell . . . to whom he said upon resigning his gown : "My lord, you must take nothing *off* it, for I'll soon need it again." To which Mr. Campbell replied, "It will be *bare enough*, Harry, before you get it." On the return of the Whigs to power, Mr. Erskine once more became Lord Advocate.' Fergusson tells also the following story : 'In his early days at Parliament House, and while passing through a stage of comparative inactivity, before his practice became absorbing, Mr. Erskine was one of the most persevering of wags. It was his special delight to tease Sir James Colquhoun of Luss, who was Principal Clerk of Session, . . . and one of the oddest characters of the time. On one occasion, while Henry Erskine was in court during the advising of an important case, he amused himself by making faces, as he sat at the clerk's table beneath the judges. The victim was naturally much annoyed by this procedure, but bore it as long as he could. At last he could stand it no longer, and disturbed the gravity of the court by rising and exclaiming—'My lord—my lord—I wish you would speak to Henry; he's aye makking faces at me.' Harry, however, was looking graver than the judges. Quiet was restored, and the advising went on, when Sir James, happening to cast his eyes towards the bar, was met by a new grimace from his tormentor, and once more convulsed the bench, bar, and audience by roaring out in his rage—"See there, my lord, he's at it again."' Erskine's eloquence and wit were so attractive to the bench, that when, on one occasion, he said, 'I shall not need to take up much of your lordship's time—I shall be very brief,' one of the judges entered a mild protest : 'Hoots, Maister Harry, dinna be

brief—dinna be brief.' He has been credited with the remark,
in reply to the assertion that punning was the *lowest* kind of
wit, that it must be the best kind, being the *foundation* of
the whole. Jeffrey said of him: 'All his wit was argument,
and each of his delightful illustrations a material step in
reasoning'; and Cockburn said: 'He reasoned in wit,' but
considered that the power was not a serviceable one, inas-
much as it 'established obstructing associations of cheerfulness, whenever he appeared, in the public mind.' Scott said
of him: 'He was the best-natured man I ever knew;
thoroughly a gentleman, and with but one fault—he could
not say *no*, and thus sometimes misled those who trusted
him.' Erskine had nothing to trouble the even flow of his
domestic life with two successive helpmates, beyond the
humour of the first for 'spending half the night in examining
the family wardrobe, and occasionally invoking her liege
lord with such appalling inquiries as, "Harry, where's your
white waistcoat?"' Erskine retired to his country seat in
1811, on being disappointed of his hopes of preferment on the
death of President Blair. It is fitting that we conclude our
notice of this amiable man and exquisite humorist by
narrating one more characteristic anecdote. A friend encountering him in the street, just after the death of one
Wright, an indifferently successful advocate, said: 'Well,
Harry, poor Johnny Wright is dead.' 'Is he?' exclaimed
Erskine. 'He died very poor; they say he left no effects.'
'That's not surprising,' was the rejoinder; 'as he had no
causes, he could have no effects.' Erskine's death occurred in
1817, at the age of seventy-one. (See ERSKINE, HENRY, p. 10.)

No. 39 was the residence at the time of his death of
DR. ALEXANDER ADAM, the writer on Roman antiquities,
and Rector of the High School; the story of whose struggles
in a lodging at fourpence a week in a small room at Restalrig
—living on oatmeal and small beans with an occasional penny
loaf, while attending the college classes—is told with some
variation by different writers. Lord Brougham, in his *Life*,
says Adam received three guineas per quarter as assistant
to Allan Maconochie in the capacity of tutor. This appears
to be an error; his remuneration, which compelled him to
the economy above detailed, having been, according to his
biographer, Henderson, only a third of that amount. Few
teachers have had as their pupils so many eminent men.
Brougham says of him: 'Dr. Adam was a teacher of the
greatest merit, and a man distinguished by qualities very
rarely found in combination with his literary eminence. His

temper was never soured, nor his spirits depressed; the zeal of studying and success in it sustaining him and even making him feel happy' (*Life of Brougham*). Scott, in his autobiography, writes : 'Dr. Adam, to whom I owed so much, never failed to remind me of my obligations when I had made some figure in the literary world. He was, indeed, deeply imbued with that fortunate vanity which alone could induce a man who has arms to pare and burn a muir to submit to the yet more toilsome task of cultivating youth. . . . He remembered the fate of every boy at his school during the fifty years he had supported it, and always traced their success or misfortunes entirely to their attention or neglect when under his care. His "noisy mansion," which to others would have been a melancholy bedlam, was the pride of his heart; and the only fatigues he felt, amid din and tumult, and the necessity of reading themes, hearing lessons, and maintaining some degree of order at the same time, were relieved by comparing himself to Cæsar, who could dictate to three secretaries at once—so ready is vanity to lighten the labours of duty' (Lockhart's *Scott*). Scott, however, attributes to 'vanity' what was undoubtedly an actual love of his occupation on the part of the good Doctor. In his last moments his thoughts, in his delirium, were with his pupils ; and just before he expired, he was heard to say : 'It grows dark, boys ; you can go ; we must do the rest to-morrow.' Henderson, his biographer, thus describes him : 'His external appearance was that of a schoolmaster, who dressed neatly for his own sake, but who had never incommoded himself with fashion in the cut of his coat or the regulation of his gait. Upon the street he often appeared in a studious attitude, and in winter always walked with his hands crossed and thrust into his sleeves. His features were regular and manly, and he was above the middle size. In his well-formed proportions, and in his prim regular face, there appeared the marks of habitual temperance.' He was accustomed to devote the vacation time of six weeks to literary work, taking no holiday, and would resort to Arthur Seat for meditation. A year before his death he frequently climbed the hill before breakfast, an extraordinary achieve- ment for a man of his age and pursuits.' He died in 1809, having reached his sixty-eighth year.

No. **45** was, in the second decade of the century, the residence of ROBERT JAMESON, Regius Professor of Natural History in the University of Edinburgh. The 'Father of modern natural history,' as he has been called, developed his tendencies as a boy when at school by stuffing birds and collecting plants and animals on the beach at Leith. His name will be ever associated with the Edinburgh Museum, which he developed out of the dilapidated and neglected remains of the bequest of Sir Andrew Balfour in 1694. His *Elements of Geognosy*—propounding the theories of Werner, which he had studied in Germany under the master, in opposition to those of Hutton—was produced during, or just before, his residence here; and the *Edinburgh Philosophical Journal* was started by him in conjunction with Brewster, towards its close, in 1819. He removed to 21 Royal Circus. Born 1772, died 1854. (See JAMESON, p. 88.)

At No. **56** died ROBERT BLAIR, Lord President of the Court of Session. 'As I was going along Maitland Street on the evening of the 20th of May 1811,' writes Lord Cockburn, 'I met Sir Henry Moncreiff, who asked me, with great agitation, if I had heard what had happened. He then told me that President Blair was dead. He had been in Court that day, apparently in good health, and had gone to take his usual walk from his house in George Square round by

56 GEORGE SQUARE.

Bruntsfield Links and the Grange, where his solitary figure had long been a known and respected object, when he was struck with sudden illness, staggered home, and died.' Of his habits R. P. Gillies (*Memoirs of a Literary Veteran*) tells us: 'If I remember right, he used to retire to rest early . . . and rose to breakfast betwixt four and five, and had half a day's work achieved before his public duties in the Court commenced;' also, 'that light reading had a great charm for his leisure hours, and he would enjoy *Gulliver's Travels* or the last new novel with all the fresh feelings of boyhood.' Cockburn says that 'he cared neither for claret nor for whisky.' Lockhart, in *Peter's Letters to his Kinsfolk*, tells how on one occasion Lord Eldin was heard to mutter between his teeth after his discomfiture in court by the President's demolition of his sophistical argument, 'My man! God almighty spared nae pains when he made your brains.' At the death of Blair, in 1811, a full civic ceremonial attended his body to the grave. He was seventy years of age.

At No. 57 lived ROBERT DUNDAS of Arniston, Chief Baron, the son of one Lord President, and the grandson of another. ' In public affairs,' says Cockburn, ' the most important person in this country ' at the time; 'for he was Lord Advocate in the most alarming times, and at a period when extravagant and arbitrary powers were ascribed to that office. . . . He was a little, alert, handsome, gentleman-like man, with a countenance and air beaming with sprightliness and gaiety, and dignified by considerable fire, although inexpressibly pleasing' (*Memorials of My Time*). He died in 1819, at the age of sixty-one.

No. 57 is very memorable also as the scene of the death of the uncle of the Chief Baron, the first LORD MELVILLE (Henry Dundas). The editor of *Kay's Edinburgh Portraits* says: ' In 1811, Lord Melville, the Principal Secretary of State for the Home Department, died in the house of his nephew, Lord Chief Baron Dundas, in George Square; having come to Edinburgh, it is believed, to attend the funeral of his old friend Lord President Blair.' Blair died in the adjoining house, No. 56. Cockburn writes: 'The first Lord Melville had retired to rest in his usual health, but was found dead in bed next morning. These two early, attached, and illustrious friends were thus lying, suddenly dead, with but a wall between them. Their houses, on the north-east side of George Square, were next each other.' Cockburn goes on to state: 'It has always been said, and never so far as I know contradicted, and I am inclined to believe it, that a letter written by him was found on his table or in a writing-case, giving a feeling account of his emotions at the President's funeral. It was a fancy piece, addressed to a member of the Government, with a view to obtain some public provision for Blair's family, and the author had not reckoned on the possibility of his own demise before his friend's funeral took place. Such things are always awkward when detected, especially when done by a skilful politician. Nevertheless, an honest and true man might do this. It is easy to anticipate one's feelings at a friend's burial; and putting the description into the form of having returned from it is mere rhetoric.' Scott in a letter in Lockhart's *Life*, writes: ' Here is a very odd coincidence between the deaths of these eminent characters and that of a very inferior person, a dentist of this city named Dubisson. He met the President before his death, who used a particular expression in speaking to him; the day before Lord Melville died, he also met Dubisson nearly on the same spot, and, to the man's surprise, used the President's very words in saluting him. On this second death he said (jocularly, however) that he apprehended that he himself would be the third—was taken ill, and died in an hour's space. Was not this remarkable!' In *Kay's Edinburgh Portraits*, it is stated that after paying the expense of his education and admission to the Faculty (of Advocates) in 1763, 'Mr. Dundas had just sixty pounds remaining of his patrimony.' It is here said of him that, 'in private life his manners were affable and unaffected, his disposition amiable and affectionate. A striking instance of the kindness of his nature is to be found in the fact that, to the latest period of his life, whenever he came to Edinburgh, he made a point of calling in person on all the old ladies with whom he had been acquainted in the days of his youth; patiently and perseveringly climbing for this purpose some of the most formidable turnpike stairs in the Old Town. In his person he was tall and well formed, while his countenance was expressive of high intellectual endowments.' A writer in the *Dictionary of National Biography* says: 'As the intimate friend and trusted lieutenant of Pitt, Lord Melville fills an important place in the political history of the age in which he lived. Without any gift of eloquence, and in spite of his broad Scotch accent and ungraceful manner, he was a steady debater, and lucid and argumentative speaker. Deficient alike in refinement and literary taste, he was possessed of great political sagacity and indefatigable industry. In his private life he was frank and straightforward in character, convivial in his habits, and utterly indifferent about money.' He died in 1811, aged seventy.

CHARLES STREET.

At No. 7 FRANCIS JEFFREY was born, in 1773. Cockburn says it was 'in one of the flats or floors of what is now marked No. 7, on the west side of Charles Street, George Square. Besides other unquestionable evidence, he himself pointed this out as his birthplace to his friend, Mr. Adam Black the bookseller' (see JEFFREY, pp. 32, 55, 63, 84, 105).

Turning to the left in Bristo Street, Teviot Place leads to
Lauriston Place: on the left of which is

LAURISTON LANE.

No. **2** was the residence, in the fifth decade of the century,
of the REV. DR. THOMAS GUTHRIE. In his interesting *Autobiography*, he says: 'Most of the ministers lived in houses
too good and costly for their incomes. I avoided this. On
removing . . . to Brown Square, and becoming next neighbour to Lord Gleenlee, I, with a small rise in the world, paid
only £39; and when I next moved out of these old-fashioned
places [he had previously lived in Argyll Square] to 2 Lauriston Lane, which was fast falling into the sere and yellow
leaf, I only paid £40.' Dr. Guthrie's appearance was most imposing. 'To his outward appearance alone he owed not a
little of his influence over others. A man nearly six feet
three inches in height, of a massive frame, broad-shouldered
and erect in bearing, he had, especially in later life, a noble
presence; a countenance beaming and shrewd, the play of
whose features was such that no picture of the many taken
ever exactly depicted it. He had a charm of manner whose
attractions none could resist; and in addition to all these
qualities, he was—what all men of an emotional temperament are not—endowed with singular sagacity and strong
common sense' (Chambers's *Biographical Dictionary*). He
died in 1873, at the age of seventy (see GUTHRIE, p. 111).

At a house in the lane, though where situate is unknown,
the REV. JOHN ERSKINE, D.D., resided. He came to Edinburgh in 1758, and in 1767 became colleague to Dr. Robertson
at New Greyfriars Church. 'No Edinburgh figure was better
known,' writes Cockburn in his *Memorials*: 'if stretched out
he might probably have been of the average height; but
during his latter years he stooped so much that he was
below it. He was one of the very few who in those days
were not deformed by hair powder, and he was distinguished by a neat, well-kept, jet-black wig, and plain but
nice raiment. His face was small, pale, and active like; his
figure that of a thin, ardent creature. Stooping so low that
it seemed as if he was looking for something on the ground,
and hirpling along, with his hands in his sides, and his
elbows turned outwards, he resembled a piece of old china
with two handles. He was all soul and no body. Never was
there such a spectre or such a spirit. There was nothing
that this man would not do for truth or for a friend.'

Erskine was frequently very absent. Wandering one day in the Links of Edinburgh, he stumbled against a cow; with his usual politeness he took off his hat, made a low bow and a thousand apologies, and walked on under the impression that he had jostled a stranger; and a story is told of his having met his wife in the meadows, who stopped on approaching him : he did so too, bowed, hoped she was well, and passed on ; and on his return home told her that he had met a lady and exchanged salutes with her, but could not imagine who she was. An illustration of his kindness of heart and simplicity of manner is narrated in the discovery of the regular theft of his pocket-handkerchief as he went up the pulpit stairs for several Sundays. Mrs. Erskine sewed the handkerchief to the coat-pocket. A gentle nibble from behind betrayed the thief in the person of a demure-looking elderly woman, who sat on the pulpit stairs. The doctor turning gently round, and 'clapping detected guilt' on the head, merely remarked, ' No the day, honest woman, no the day.' Sir H. Moncreiff Wellwood, in his *Account of the Life and Writings of Dr. Erskine*, says : ' His faculties were so entire, and such was his literary perseverance to the end, that on the very night before he died he was eagerly employed reading a new Dutch book, of which the leaves had been till then uncut.' He died in 1803, at the age of eighty-one.

The next turning in Lauriston Place after Lauriston Lane is

ARCHIBALD PLACE.

At No. **16,** while editor of *The Witness*—for which post he was brought from his bank desk to Edinburgh in 1840—lived HUGH MILLER. The writer of the memoir in Chambers's *Biographical Dictionary* says : 'Even in childhood he had been an enthusiast, and his enthusiasm had been of that unhealthy kind which sees ghosts, and devoutly believes in omens and prodigies . . . Little did the public guess, when he walked among them, one of the most honoured and distinguished of the day—when his shaggy head was still brown, and his athletic strength in the prime of manhood, that the stalwart intellectual stone-mason whose grey plaid and russet attire, which he wore to the last, and whom strangers in Princes Street looked at in wonderment when they were assured that this was the world-famed Hugh Miller—little did the public guess that all this glory, and freshness, and true worth were accompanied with a jarring nerve in the

brain under which all availed him nothing.' Miller afterwards removed to Portobello (see MILLER, p. 109).
  At the end of Lauriston Place is

LAURISTON STREET.

At No. 15, removed to make room for the chapel, but of a
character corresponding to the adjoining house which remains,
at the time of his death lived DAVID SCOTT, 'the poet-painter,
whose life was a feverish struggle with great conceptions,
and whose artistic productions showed that, had his life been
continued, he might have embodied those conceptions in
paintings that would have created a new school of art. Of
him it may truly be said that a generation must yet pass
away, and a new world of living men enter into their room,
before his talents are fully appreciated, and their place
distinctly assigned' (Chambers's *Biographical Dictionary*).
It has been said of him that: 'With all his professional
faults and moral peculiarities, David Scott was a painter of
great power and ability, and by his constant perseverance
in the line he had proposed for himself, in spite of almost
constant disappointment, proved himself a true artist if a
mistaken man. Incessant hope deferred preyed upon his
constitution, and carried him to a premature grave.' He died
in the year 1848, aged forty-two (see SCOTT p. 103).

ROUTE III.

THE NEW TOWN.

WE take our departure from the Post-Office, at the eastern end of

PRINCES STREET.

No. 10 was the shop of ARCHIBALD CONSTABLE, the famous publisher. It has been much altered, and is now a glass and china warehouse with hotel above. Constable removed hither in 1822, having acquired the premises by purchase from the connections of his second marriage. His rise from the position of a lad in Hill's shop to the head of the publishing and bookselling trade in Edinburgh had been extraordinarily rapid. Cockburn writes: 'Abandoning the old timid, grudging system, he stood out as the general patron and payer of all promising publications; and confounded not merely his rivals in

10 PRINCES STREET.

the trade, but his very authors, by his unheard-of prices. Ten, even twenty, guineas a sheet for a review; £2000 or £3000 for a single poem, and £1000 each for two philosophical dissertations, drew authors from dens where they would otherwise have starved, and made Edinburgh a literary mart famous with strangers, and the pride of its own citizens' (*Memorials*). 'Proceeding in this manner,' says a writer in Chambers's *Biographical Dictionary*, 'rather like a princely patron of letters than a tradesman aiming at making them subservient to his personal interest, Mr. Constable was easily led into a system of living greatly beyond his real means. With Scott he launched, without rudder or compass, into an ocean of bank credit, in which they were destined eventually to perish.' Lockhart describes him as 'a good-looking man, ... very fat in his person, but with a face with good lines, and a fine, healthy complexion. He is one of the most jolly-looking members of the trade I ever saw; and moreover one of the most pleasing and courtly in his address' (*Peter's Letters*). Constable survived his financial troubles but a year, dying of dropsy at his house in Park Place—no longer existing—in 1827, at the early age of fifty-three (see p. 105).

No. 17, which like No. 10 has undergone 'structural altera-tion,' is memorable as the birthplace of *Blackwood's Maga-zine*, and place of business of its enterprising proprietor and editor, WILLIAM BLACKWOOD. Chambers (*Walks in Edinburgh*, 1829) refers to the premises as forming 'the lounge and resort of the principal Tory literati.' Lockhart, describing his introduction to the great bookseller in the character of Peter Morris says: 'Stimulated and supported by the example and success of John Murray, whose agent he is, he determined to make, if possible, Princes Street to the High Street what the other has made Albemarle Street to the Row . . . . The length of vista presented to one on enter-ing the shop has a very imposing effect; for it is carried back, room after room, through various gradations of light and shadow, till the eye cannot see distinctly the outline of any object in the furthest distance. First there is, as usual, a special place set apart for retail business . . . . Then you have an elegant oval saloon, lighted from the roof, where various groups of loungers and literary dilettanti are engaged in looking at, or criticising amongst themselves, the publications just arrived by that day's coach from town' (*Peter's Letters*). The reference to the oval saloon, no longer existing, seems to have misled Grant (*Old and New Edin-burgh*) into misapplying this description to the later and present premises of the firm in George Street, where there is a fine circular vestibule. A bookselling business is now car-ried on at the Princes Street premises (see BLACKWOOD, pp. 54, 84, 111).

South St. Andrew Street leads to

ST. ANDREW SQUARE.

At No. 2, now part of an hotel, died DR. JAMES GREGORY, successor to Dr. Cullen as Professor of the Practice of Physic in the University of Edinburgh in 1790, a position which he retained until his death thirty-one years after. 'During this long period,' we read in Chambers's *Biographical Dictionary*, 'the fame which his talents had acquired attracted students to Edinburgh from all parts of the world; all of whom returned to their homes with a feeling of reverence for his character more nearly resembling that which the disciples of antiquity felt for their instructors than anything which is generally experienced in the present state of society.' 'Descended by the father's side,' says the same authority, 'from a long and memorable line of ancestors; and by the mother's from one of the oldest baronial families in the country, the character of Dr. Gregory was early formed upon an elevated model, and throughout his whole life he combined in a manner seldom equalled the studies and acquisitions of a man of science with the tastes and honourable feeling of a high-born gentleman.' It has to be admitted, however, by the candid biographer, that some pamphlets on the management of the College of Surgeons which he issued indicate in their spirit and manner 'a most striking view of one of the paradoxes occasionally to be found in human character; the co-existence in the same bosom of sentiments of chivalrous honour and benevolence with the most inveterate hostility towards individuals.' Dr. Gregory was sixty-eight at the time of his death in 1821.

No. **21**, at the corner of North St. David Street, is universally regarded as having been the residence of DAVID STEWART ERSKINE, EARL OF BUCHAN, and corresponds to the description to be presently quoted in Lord Brougham's *Life* as 'No. 21 north side' of the square. Moreover, the house is so numbered on Kirkwood's Plan of Edinburgh, 1790. But it is remarkable that Chambers (*Walks in Edinburgh*) refers to Lord Buchan's residence as 'the house at the end of the north side to the east,' and Fergusson (*Life of Henry Erskine*) as 'No. 27, the corner house looking into North

21 ST. ANDREW SQUARE.

St. Andrew Street.' But Chambers also speaks of it as No. 21, which would seem to imply that he wrote 'east' for 'west,' and that Fergusson copied the error, while Fergusson's *impossible* number (27) may have been a printer's blunder. In 1780 the establishment of the Society of Scottish Antiquarians, which Lord Buchan originated, was finally determined on at a meeting at his house. The noble Earl stands out prominently as an 'eccentric' of his time. 'He was really good-tempered, well-meaning, and kind-hearted after his own fashion,' writes R. P. Gillies (*Reminiscences of a Literary Veteran*) 'exhibiting the strangest compound I had ever known of learning and talent with wayward vanity and eccentricity. . . . He rose early, went out in all weathers, despised luxury in his own *ménage*, and was perpetually at work, or on the alert, from six in the morning till twelve at night. . . . But, alas! his lordship's works did not turn to much account or profit, and his vivacity was too great in its degree.' He was a contributor to *The Gentleman's Magazine* and to *The Bee*; and wrote an essay on the poet Thomson, in honour of whom he instituted an annual festival at the birthplace of the poet, Ednam, in Roxburghshire; while he erected a Grecian temple in his own grounds at Dryburgh, with a statue of Apollo inside and a bust of Thomson on the top of the dome. 'His relation to art and letters,' to quote the *Dictionary of National Biography*, 'was in great part that of a fussy and intermeddling patron.' Horace Walpole found him a bore as a correspondent, and says in his *Letters* that he 'tried everything without being rude to break off the intercourse,' and he wanted to be admitted to Scott's bed-chamber when he was ill in 1819, 'to communicate his arrangements about his funeral,' having previously prevailed on Scott to accept as a burial-place the sepulchral aisles of Scott's Haliburton ancestors in Dryburgh. As it happened, Scott was the first to fill the office of mourner. The classical mania by which he was afflicted led him, according to Gillies, into a freak which 'drew on him the ridicule of the town.' On the occasion of one of his breakfast parties, he selected nine young ladies of rank, who were to personate the nine Muses, whilst he himself received them in the character of Apollo. The young ladies and their illustrious host were in fancy dresses, but unluckily the classic models had, in one instance, been too closely observed, for when Cupid entered with the tea-kettle, he had no dress whatsoever. Hereupon the young ladies were so much amazed that they all started up, and, tittering and screaming, ran out of the room.' No doubt the noble host carried his own costume with good

D

effects. The artists were constantly at work on him. Lockhart says : ' I do not remember to have seen a more exquisite
old head. . . . The features are all perfect, but the greatest
beauty is in the clear blue eyes, which are chased in his head
in a way that might teach something to the best sculptor in
the world ' (*Peter's Letters to his Kinsfolk*). Born 1742. Died
1829.

But No. 21 possesses a stronger interest than that attaching
to the residence of this eccentric nobleman, as the birth-place
of HENRY, LORD BROUGHAM. In his mother's ' Notes,' prefixed to his own *Life and Times*, we read : ' He went to
school on the 19th September 1785, having been born on that
day in the year 1778, at No. 21, north side of St. Andrew
Square.' Brougham himself tells how his father was ' con-
signed ' by his friends to the care of Lord Buchan, ' who
lived sometimes at Dryburgh Abbey and sometimes in Edinburgh,' ' in the hopes that, introduced by him to the best
Edinburgh society, he might find occupation and distraction
enough to mitigate his grief '—the ' grief ' being for the loss
of his intended bride, Mary Whelpdale, who died the day
before that fixed for the wedding. ' Accordingly to Edinburgh he went, and there, among other distinguished persons,
made the acquaintance of Dr. Robertson, at whose house he
met his eldest sister, then a widow, and her only child
Eleanor. This acquaintance ended in a marriage, and then
my father and his bride moved to St. Andrew Square, to the
house in which Lord and Lady Buchan lived, and there I
was born on the 19th of September 1778 ' (see BROUGHAM,
p. 26).

No. 8 is memorable as the house in which DAVID HUME
spent his later years, and where he died. It is definitely
described by Robert Chambers in *Walks in Edinburgh* ' as
the extreme western house upon the south side of St.
Andrew Square, entering from St. David Street. . . . at
present occupied by a fashionable Schneider.' Burton (*Life
of Hume*) says : ' When the house was built and inhabited
by Hume, but while yet the street, of which it was the
commencement, had no name, a witty young lady, daughter
of Baron Ord, chalked on the wall the words " St. David
Street." The allusion was obvious. Hume's lass, judging
that it was not meant in honour or reverence, ran into the
house, much excited, to tell her master how he was made
game of. " Never mind, lassie," he said, " many a better
man has been made a saint of before." ' On this story,

Chambers remarks: 'Perhaps if it be presumed that a corresponding street at the other angle of St. Andrew Square is called St. Andrew Street, a natural enough circumstance with reference to the square, whose title was determined on the plan, it will appear likely that the choosing of St. David Street for that in which Hume's house stood was not originally designed as a jest at his expense, though a second thought, and the whim of his friends might quickly give it that application' (*Traditions of Edinburgh*). Hume was very corpulent in his later years. In Dr. Carlyle's *Autobiography* he is referred to as a 'large jolly man' by Mrs. Adam—mother of the famous

8 ST. ANDREW SQUARE.

architect, Robert Adam—who found him 'the most innocent, agreeable, facetious man she ever met with,' and was astonished to find she had been entertaining, by a cunning device of her son, the identical 'Atheist' whom she had expressly excepted from the guests who might visit her house. Boswell tells of a good well-meaning lady-member of a dissenting congregation who called on Hume at the commencement of his last illness to talk to him about religion, and, though a stranger to him, was admitted, and courteously invited to take a glass of wine, and who went away without fulfilling her self-imposed mission, owing to her eagerness to inform her husband of a very large order for *candles*, with which Hume, hearing he was a chandler, had entrusted her. He died in the year 1776, at the age of sixty-five, from a disorder of the bowels, of which hæmorrhage was a prominent feature; but which is said not only to have caused him no pain, but developed itself in connection with so positively *enjoyable* an existence, that Hume compared it favourably with his experience of any previous period of his life. Hume was born 1711, and died 1776 (see HUME, pp. 2, 5, 19).

PRINCES STREET.

At No. **79**—formerly, like all the houses in the chief streets
of the New Town, a private residence—lived DR. THOMAS
BROWN (less noteworthy in connection with his degree of
M.D. than as one of the earliest contributors to the *Edinburgh
Review*, and as Professor Dugald Stewart's colleague and
successor in the Chair of Moral Philosophy in Edinburgh
University). His powers were displayed at a præternaturally
early age in a critical comparison of the four gospels when
he was only four years old. His biographer, the Rev. David
Welsh, describes him as 'in height rather above the middle
size, about five feet nine inches, his chest broad and round,
his hair brown, his forehead large and prominent, his eyes
dark grey and well-formed, with very long eyelashes . . . His
nose might be said to be a mixture of the Roman and
Grecian, and his mouth and chin bore a striking resemblance
to those of the Buonaparte family. . . . In private life he was
possessed of almost every quality which renders society
delightful, and was, indeed, remarkable for nothing more
than for the love of home and the happiness he shed around
him there.' From 1806 Dr. Brown was in partnership with
Dr. Gregory. He writes to him from here in January 1820;
before the year was out, a constitution always delicate had
given way. He died at Brompton, London, on his way to the
south of Europe. Born 1778; died 1820.

No. **93** was the residence for a long period of CHARLES
KIRKPATRICK SHARPE. 'I called upon him,' writes Chambers
(*Traditions of Edinburgh*), 'at his mother's house, No. 93
Princes Street, in a somewhat excited frame of mind. His
servant conducted me to the first floor, and showed me into
what is generally called amongst us the back drawing-room.'
The same writer thus describes him: 'His thin effeminate
figure, his voice pitched in *alt*, his attire, as he took his daily
walks in Princes Street, a long blue frock coat, black trousers,
rather wide below, and sweeping over white stockings and
neat shoes—something like a web of white cambric round
his neck, and a brown wig coming down to his eyebrows—
had long established him as what is called a character.' He
appears to have been living here as late as 1835. He was
born 1780; died 1851 (see SHARPE, p. 95).

No. **108** is associated with two different names—father and
son. LORD WOODHOUSELEE was the senatorial title assumed

in 1805 by ALEXANDER FRASER TYTLER, chiefly distinguished as professor of History. Cockburn says he was 'no lawyer . . . unquestionably a person of correct taste, a cultivated mind, and literary habits, and very amiable . . . but there is no kindness in insinuating that he was a man of genius, and of public or even social influence.' Sir Archibald Alison, in a *Memoir* of him, says: 'A more warm-hearted, refined, and accomplished man never existed than this ornament of the Scottish Bar, and afterwards of the Scottish Bench. His abilities were of a very superior order, but they were of the contemplative and retiring rather than of the active and enterprising kind.' He died 1813, aged eighty-five.

PATRICK FRASER TYTLER, son of Lord Woodhouselee, left Edinburgh for London on his wife's death in 1834. His *History of Scotland* was completed nine years later. Sir Archibald Alison calls him 'a delightful companion,' and remarks on the 'mingled talent, fun, and simplicity of his character' (*Autobiography*). Of a singularly buoyant and happy temperament, it is said that he 'mesmerised the company for the time into being as happy as himself.' He died prematurely, after many years of sickness and suffering, in 1849, aged fifty-eight.

No. 108 is now a confectioner's, and is noteworthy as the first of the Princes Street houses west of Hanover Street converted into business premises. Tea, coffee, and ices are now consumed in Lord Woodhouselee's drawing-room, of which Lord Woodhouselee's daughter writes: 'Well do I remember the drawing-room in Princes Street, with its mirrors between the windows, and the large round tea-table in the middle of the room—that tea-table which recalled such glorious tea-drinkings, when Walter Scott, Dugald Stewart, Playfair, Henry Mackenzie, Sydney Smith, and other intimate friends sat around it.'—(*Memoir of Patrick Fraser Tytler*).

We leave Princes Street at South Frederick Street, crossing George Street into

NORTH FREDERICK STREET.

At No. 36, now in the possession of several business firms, PERCY BYSSHE SHELLEY lodged on his second visit to Edinburgh, with his wife and infant, in 1813. In a note to Professor Dowden's *Life of Shelley*, we read : 'They stayed at 36 Frederick Street. Mr. Rossetti writes: "In August Shelley came of age, and his first act was to marry Harriet over again in an Episcopal church in Edinburgh." He adds a note : "This detail which I give in the words of an informant extremely unlikely to be mistaken, has never hitherto been recorded ; and the journey to Edinburgh has passed as being one of Shelley's motiveless and costly freaks." I find no reference to such a marriage in letters from Edinburgh, in which I think it would have been mentioned had it taken place. Certainly when Shelley started on his journey he had no intention of visiting Edinburgh. His motive in the expedition, I surmise, was to escape from the pressure of creditors, while paying a portion of his debts with the money raised on the *post-obit* bond, and expecting to come to an arrangement with his father.' Shelley died in 1822 at the age of thirty.

GEORGE STREET.

No. **45** is famous in the present as in the past as the publishing house of MESSRS. BLACKWOOD. William Blackwood removed hither from Princes Street about 1830. Sir Theodore Martin, in his *Life of Aytoun*, refers to the handsome circular vestibule in the rear as hung with portraits of contributors to the Magazine. It now contains an admirable portrait of Sir Theodore himself (see BLACKWOOD, pp. 47, 84, 111).

At No. **46** SYDNEY SMITH was living in 1802-3, when engaged in 'superintending,' to use Lord Brougham's phrase, or, as Sydney Smith himself called it, 'editing' the first number of the *Edinburgh Review*. In 1797 he went to London. Altogether he resided about six years in Edinburgh ; in 1800 we find him living at 79 Queen Street, and when Robert Chambers met him in London many years later, and asked him where he had resided in Edinburgh, he is reported to have said, 'In Buccleuch Street, not far from Jeffrey's, with an outlook on the Meadows.' To the number in Buccleuch Street, however, we have no clue. In person, Sydney Smith was 'of a portly figure,' writes Mr. S. C. Hall, 'stout, indeed clumsy, with a healthy look, and a self-enjoying aspect. He was rapid in movement as well as in words, and evidently studied more ease than dignity.' He died in 1845, at the age of seventy-four (see SMITH, p. 62).

At No. 75 lived Mrs. SCOTT, the mother of Sir Walter Scott, and here she died in 1819. The lower part is now a wine merchant's and a milliner's.

To No. 92 FRANCIS JEFFREY removed from Queen Street in 1810. Cockburn describes it as 'a small house occupied entirely by himself.' Here he resided seventeen years. Lockhart's description of him in *Peter's Letters to his Kinsfolk* may find a fitting place here: 'It is a face which any man would pass without observation in a crowd, because it is small and swarthy, and entirely devoid of lofty or commanding outlines; and besides, his stature is so low that he might walk close under your chin or mine, without catching the eye even for a moment. . . . The forehead is very singularly shaped, describing in its bend from side to side a larger segment of a circle than is at all common, compressed below the temples almost as much as Sterne's, and throwing out sinuses above the eyes of an extremely bold and compact structure. The hair is very black and wiry, standing in ragged bristling clumps out from the upper part of his head, but lying close and firm lower down, especially about the ears. . . . The lips are very firm, but they tremble and vibrate, even when brought close together, in such a way as to give the idea of an intense, never-ceasing play of mind. . . . But what speaking things are his eyes!' Cockburn, contrasting Jeffrey with Scott, says: 'He was sharp English; with few anecdotes and no stories, delighting in the interchange of minds, bright in moral speculation, wit, and colloquial eloquence, and always beloved for the constant transportation of an affectionate and cheerful heart.' Carlyle said: 'Jeffrey was a Benthamite on the surface, and underneath an Epicurean, with a good-humoured contempt for enthusiasm and high aspirations' (Froude's *Carlyle*). Carlyle first made the acquaintance of Jeffrey here very shortly before the latter removed to Moray Place in 1827. Carlyle says in his *Reminiscences*: 'I got ready admission into Jeffrey's study, or rather "office," for it had mostly that air: a roomy, not over neat apartment on the ground floor, with a big baize-covered table loaded with book-rows and paper bundles . . . five pairs of candles were cheerfully burning, in the light of which sate my famous little gentleman; laid aside his work,—cheerfully invited me to sit, and began talking in a perfectly human manner.' Jeffrey was born in 1773, died 1850 (see JEFFREY, pp. 32, 42, 63, 84, 105).

NORTH CASTLE STREET.

No. 39 is ever memorable as the home of SIR WALTER SCOTT. He came here, after a temporary residence at a

house in South Castle Street, soon after his marriage, and in the year 1798. Writing of him in 1811, Lord Cockburn says, in his *Memorials*: 'People used to be divided at this time as to the superiority of Scott's poetry or his talk. His novels had not yet begun to suggest another alternative. Scarcely, however, even in his novels, was he more striking or delightful than in society; where the halting limb, the burr in the throat, the heavy cheeks, the high Goldsmith forehead, the unkempt locks, and general plainness of appearance, with the Scotch accent,

39 NORTH CASTLE STREET.

and stories, and sayings, all graced by gaiety, simplicity and kindness, made a combination most worthy of being enjoyed.' 'He was a most extraordinary being,' says Hogg; 'how or when he composed his voluminous works no man could tell. When in Edinburgh he was bound to the Parliament House all the forenoon. He never was denied to any living lady or gentleman, poor or rich, and he never seemed discomposed when intruded on; but always good-humoured and kind. Many a time have I been sorry for him, for I have remained in his study in Castle Street in hopes to get a quiet word out of him, and witnessed the admission of ten intruders forby myself' (*Domestic Manners and Private Life of Scott*). Captain Basil Hall writes in his diary in 1826, 'five months after the total ruin' of Scott's 'pecuniary fortunes, and twenty-six days after the death of his wife': 'In the days of his good-luck he used to live at No. 39 North Castle Street, in a house befitting a rich baronet; but on reaching the door I found the plate on it covered with rust (so soon is glory obscured), the windows shuttered up, dirty and comfortless; and from the side of one projected a

board "To sell." The stairs were unwashed, and not a foot-
mark told of the ancient hospitality which reigned within.
In all nations with which I am acquainted, the fashionable
world move westward, in imitation, perhaps, of the greater
tide of civilisation; and *vice versa*, those persons who decline
in fortune, which is mostly equivalent to declining in fashion,
shape their course eastward. Accordingly, by an involun-
tary impulse, I turned my head that way, and, inquiring
at the Clubs in Princes Street, learned that he now resided
in St. David Street, No. 6.' Of Scott's health at one part
of this period, in 1819, a significant intimation occurs in a
letter to Constable, given in *Archibald Constable and his
Literary Correspondents*: 'Last night was a cruelly painful
trial, the spasms lasting from half-past six till half-past four in
the morning, without a moment's intermission, yet, after all
this agony, and much bleeding and blistering, and dosing
with laudanum, here I am sitting quietly in my own room,
in hopes, two days will restore me the use of my arms—
sorely mangled with lancets and the free exercise of my
faculties.' Lockhart describes Scott's study as having 'a
single Venetian window opening on a patch of turf not much
larger than itself, and the aspect of the place was sombrous.
. . . The only table was a massive piece of furniture which
he had constructed on the model of one at Rokeby, with a desk
and all its appurtenances on either side, that an amanuensis
might work opposite to him when he chose. . . . His own
writing apparatus was a very handsome old box richly
carved, and lined with crimson velvet. . . . The room had no
space for pictures, except one, an original portrait of Claver-
house, which hung over the chimney-piece, with a Highland
target on either side, and broadswords and dirks (each
having its own story) dispersed star fashion round them.'
Scott resided here twenty-eight years, his appointment at the
Parliament House yielding him an income of about £1500 a
year. A small bust over the door, seen through the fan-
light, is the only indication to the casual passer-by, that he
is gazing on one of the most memorable houses in the world,
(see SCOTT, *post* and pp. 33, 66, 74, 75).

SOUTH CASTLE STREET.

No. 10, as the writer is assured by Mr. David Douglas, the
publisher, of Castle Street, on undoubted authority in his
possession, is the house in which SIR WALTER SCOTT resided
for a short time before removing to North Castle Street.
Grant (*Old and New Edinburgh*) says it was No. 19.

Returning to

GEORGE STREET.

No. **108** takes us back to the period of SIR WALTER SCOTT'S first quitting the paternal roof in George Square, when he came to lodge in this house; and hither he brought his newly married wife, whose custom, as Lockhart tells, of using the best rooms for sitting in on ordinary days so shocked the landlady. The house is unchanged except in respect of a recent alteration in the entrance.

At No. **128** lived, from 1817 to 1832, SIR JAMES HALL, the results of whose scientific experiments, in association with Dr. Hutton, are to be found in the *Transactions* of the Royal Society of Edinburgh for 1806, and of his architectural theories in the *Origin, Principles, and History of Gothic Architecture*, theories illustrated in his life-time by the erection of a Gothic building constructed of twigs and boughs. In Lord Cockburn's *Memorials of My Time*, we read: 'His large house in George Street was distinguished by its hospitality both to science and fashion. And the interest of his many evening parties was not lessened by the stories of his oddities, which were sure to make the morning laugh. . . . His only misfortune was a bad manner; at least if it be a misfortune for a clever man to be much laughed at. Neither obtrusive, nor dull, nor coarse, but rather kind, gentle, and cheerful, he said and did whatever occurred to him; and as he had the always diverting defect of absence of mind, there was seldom any saying what might occur to him. There was no intentional disregard of the ordinary ceremonies of politeness; but an unconsciousness of their existence. . . . He made but one speech in Parliament, and I have heard him say that he was not much discomposed by the laughter of the whole members, but that he began to suspect that he must be making a queer figure when he saw the Speaker laugh too. It was a doubt in the family when he was a boy whether he was to turn out a man of genius or an idiot; and being in London, he was taken to the top of St. Paul's, where some one, on the hopeful side, was certain he would disclose himself by some burst of wonder. It was long of coming; but at last he screamed with delight, "Ee! there's a cuddie!" What better could a sensible boy have observed?' Sir James Hall died here after an illness extending over three and a half years, in the year 1832, at the age of seventy-one.

No. **133** was the residence of the Misses Sinclair of Ulbster.
One of these ladies was CATHERINE SINCLAIR, a novelist of
vast popularity in her day, and one of whose works, *Beatrice*,
is said to have had a sale within a few months in America
of 100,000 copies, a demand surpassing that even of *Uncle
Tom's Cabin* in England. She is memorable, however, not
only for her writings, but for her deeds of benevolence in
Edinburgh. Cooking depots were first introduced by her,
where, for sums varying from 7d. to 3½d., a comfortable
dinner could be obtained. She erected the first public
fountain in the city, and the cabmen's shelters were due
to her philanthropic exertions. She died at Kensington,
aged sixty-four, in the year 1864. It is recorded of her father,
Sir John Sinclair, whom Kay calls 'The Scottish Patriot,'
apparently because he produced a popular *Code of Agricul-
ture*, that he playfully designated the pavement in front of
his house in George Street 'The Giants' Causeway,' in
allusion to the great stature of his *thirteen* sons and
daughters.

At the end of George Street, on the south side, is

SOUTH CHARLOTTE STREET.

No. **4** was the residence of the REV. ROBERT SMITH
CANDLISH, D.D., theological writer, and the ruling spirit,
in his day, of the Free Church. He succeeded Dr. Chalmers
on the death of the latter in the Chair of Divinity in New
College. His degree was an American one, bestowed by
Princeton College, New Jersey. His life as 'minister,
church leader, and theological writer in one' was a busy life ;
but records of it contain few particulars of his personal
characteristics or habits of life. He died in 1873, at the age
of sixty-seven.

CHARLOTTE SQUARE.

At No. **9**, JAMES SYME, the celebrated surgeon, lived
from 1837 to 1842, when he removed to Millbank. 'He had
occupied several houses in town,' says Paterson (*Life of
Syme*), 'and latterly was settled in Charlotte Street, where
he married for the second time.' He is described as a man
of simple habits, 'a sincere Christian, natural in his manners,
and of gentlemanly bearing, upright in his dealings, and
genial and hospitable in the domestic circle.' Unlike members of his profession generally, 'he never noted down any
engagement, however long the interval that might elapse
before seeing the patient, and it used to be matter of

astonishment to his medical friends to see him turn up at
the precise hour, eight or nine days after he had promised
to see the case again. . . . He arranged in his own mind the
work of the day, and those visits to patients at distant
intervals of time, although never noted, were treated in
some peculiar way in his own memory.' In 1848 Syme went
to London, but found his appointment at the London University uncongenial, and returned to Edinburgh in three
months. In 1850 he was made President of the Royal College
of Surgeons of Edinburgh. His death took place in 1870; he
was seventy-one years of age (see SYME, p. 62).

At No. **14** lived for many years, about 1812-30, HENRY
COCKBURN, afterwards Lord Cockburn. 'Of all the great

pleaders of the Scottish Bar,
Mr. Cockburn is the only
one who is capable of touching, with a bold and assured
hand, the chords of feeling,
who can by one plain word
and one plain look, convey
the whole soul of tenderness
or appeal, with the authority
of a true prophet, to yet
higher emotions which
slumber in many bosoms,
but are dead, I think, in
none.' Such is the testi-
mony of his contemporary
Lockhart to Cockburn's
merits as an advocate
(*Peter's Letters to his Kins-*

14 CHARLOTTE SQUARE.

folk). Dr. Guthrie (*Memoir*) says: 'Cockburn was a man of
fascinating manners and fine genius; the greatest orator,
in one sense, I ever heard. His looks, his tones, his
language, his whole manner, were such as to make you
believe for the time that he spoke *ab imo pectore*—he
himself believing every word he said.' Lockhart thus
describes his personal appearance: 'It is, I think, a
thousand pities that this gentleman should wear a wig
in pleading; for when he throws off that incumbrance, and
appears in his natural shape, nothing can be finer than the
form of his head. He is quite bald, and his is one of the
foreheads which, in spite of antiquity, are the better for
wanting hair. . . . His face, also, is of a very striking kind
—pale and oval in its outline, having the nose perfectly

aquiline, although not very large—the mouth rather wide, but, nevertheless, firm and full of meaning—the eyes beautifully shaped, in colour of a rich clear brown, and capable of conveying a greater range of expression than almost any I have seen.' Cockburn was below the middle height. Socially, he was one of the most popular of Scotsmen, owing to his genial familiarity with men of all classes. Carlyle writes in his journal: 'In all respects the converse or contrast of Wilson; rustic Scotch sense, sincerity of humour, all of the practical Scotch types, . . . Cockburn, small, solid and genuine, was by much the wholesomer product; a bright, cheery-voiced, large-eyed man, a Scotch dialect with plenty of good logic in it, and plenty of practical sagacity; veracious too. A gentleman, I should say, perfectly in the Scotch type, perhaps the very last of that peculiar species. Cockburn was raised to the Bench in 1834. His latter years were chiefly spent at his country residence of Bonaly, near Colinton, where he died in 1854, aged seventy-five (see COCKBURN, p. 76).

Glenfinlas Street leads to

ST. COLME STREET.

To No. 7 SIR ARCHIBALD ALISON removed from his father's house (see p. 91) in 1825, on his marriage. 'In 1825,' he writes, 'we took possession of a new house which I had built in St. Colme Street, Edinburgh, one of the best situations in the town. . . . The furnishing of the house was a source of interest to us both, and many were the expeditions we made together in quest of the little niceties which add so much to the comfort without materially augmenting the expense of a dwelling.' Alison possessed great amiability of character, combined with a pleasant conviction of his own merits, as apparent in his *Autobiography*. He preserved his health by giving up writing after dinner on the completion of his *History* in 1842; and five years before his death, at the age of seventy-five, walked, as he records, twenty miles in five hours without fatigue. He wrote his book on *Population* here. 'It was at eleven at night,' he says, 'sitting in the drawing-room in St. Colme Street beside Mrs. Alison, that it was finished.' Four volumes of *The History of Europe*, written, Disraeli said, to show that 'Providence was on the side of the Tories,' were also produced here, that work being completed at Possil House, near Glasgow, whither he removed on his appointment as Sheriff of Lanarkshire in 1835, and where he died after a day's illness in 1867.

At No. **8** CAPTAIN BASIL HALL was residing in 1831. Apart from his brilliant and entertaining records of travel, and his famous *Abbotsford Journal*, Basil Hall must be ever held in kindly remembrance as having procured for Scott the offer of a Government frigate to convey him to the Mediterranean, and his tender care and solicitude for his comfort on embarking. He died at Portsmouth in 1844, at the age of fifty-six.

At the end of St. Colme Street on the north is

FORRES STREET.

No. **3**. The REV. DR. CHALMERS was living here prior to his residence in Inverleith Row, 1831-35 (see CHALMERS, pp. 107, 117).

No. **2** is now part of a hotel, and, with the former entrance removed, was the residence 1835-37 of the eminent surgeon, JAMES SYME. He removed from here to Charlotte Square (see SYME, p. 59).

QUEEN STREET

is in a line with St Colme Street.

In No. **79**, now a shop, SYDNEY SMITH was residing in 1800. He had then been three years in Edinburgh, having

79 QUEEN STREET.

been driven by stress of political troubles and the disturbed condition of the continent to abbreviate his travels in company with his pupil, Mr. Beach (the son of an ancestor of the present Sir Michael Hicks Beach), Edinburgh was chosen as an alternative residence for tutor and pupil. Sydney Smith sometimes preached at this time in Charlotte Chapel, Rose Street. Two years later we meet with him in George Street, the guiding spirit of the new *Edinburgh Review*. Although Smith exercised his wit occasionally on Scotland and the Scotch—calling the former 'the garret of the earth,' and 'the knuckle end of England,' and joking on the supposed inability of the latter to appreciate a joke—yet, as his daughter, Lady Holland, records, he always entertained a sincere affection for the country and the people. When preaching in Edinburgh, seeing how almost exclusively the congregations were made up of ladies, he once took for his text the verse, 'O that men therefore would praise the Lord,' and, with that touch of the facetious which marked everything he did, laid the emphasis on the word men (see SMITH, p. 54).

At No. 62 FRANCIS (LORD) JEFFREY was living at the memorable period of the actual commencement of the *Edinburgh Review.* 'He had third-rate apartments in a "land" situated in Queen Street. . . . Its arrangements were not symmetrical, nor indicated much attention to comfort' (R. P. Gillies, *Memoirs of a Literary Veteran*). 'Lord Jeffrey was no ordinary personage. His standing was high, both as a public man, and in the qualities which grace the more private intercourse of social life. There seemed to be a measure of his own sprightly and vivacious temperament communicated to those highly polished and intellectual *réunions* where he delighted to relax himself sometimes, as well as among the fashionable and the gay. Wonderful was the ease with which he could mix business and pleasure. Without neglecting the serious realities of life, and diligent attention to professional duties in the Parliament House, during a long summer's day, he could find time in the afternoon to attend consultations and receive clients, write law pleadings, dine out, attend his evening parties, flutter with the lively and the gay, pay homage to beauty, till the night was far spent, and then return home to write an article for a *Review*, until the morning light found him still awake and working in his study' (*Archibald Constable and his Literary Correspondents*). His wife died during his residence here, in 1805 (see JEFFREY, pp. 32, 42, 55, 84, 105).

At No. 62 also lived, from about 1824 till his death, SIR JOHN LESLIE, successor to Playfair as Professor of Natural Philosophy in the University of Edinburgh, and author of *Essay on the Nature and Properties of Heat.* Macvey Napier says of him: 'Though he did not shine in mixed society, and was latterly unfitted by a considerable degree of deafness from enjoying it, his conversation, when seated with one or two, was highly entertaining. It had no wit, little repartee, and no fine turns of any kind, but it had a strongly original and racy cast, and was replete with striking remarks and curious information. . . . He had prejudices of which it would have been better to be rid; he was not over charitable in his view of human virtue, and he was not quite so ready, on all occasions, to do that justice to a kindred merit as was to be expected in so ardent a worshipper of genius. But his faults were far more than compensated by his many good qualities—by his constant equanimity, his cheerfulness, his simplicity of character almost infantine, his straightforwardness, his perfect freedom from affectation, and, above all, his unconquerable good nature.' 'The person of Sir John Leslie,' says a writer in Chambers's *Biographical Dictionary*, 'was in later life far from gainly. He was short and corpulent with a florid face and somewhat unsightly projection of the front teeth, and tottered considerably in walking. He was, moreover, very slovenly in his mode of dressing —a peculiarity the more curious, as it was accompanied by no inconsiderable a share of *self-respect*, and an anxiety to be thought young and engaging.' He was unmarried. He died from erysipelas supervening upon a severe cold, the effects of a foolish disregard of common caution, in persistently exposing himself in the grounds at his country place in bad weather, in 1832, his age being sixty-six.

At No. 53 JOHN WILSON resided, in the house of his mother, previously to removing to Gloucester Place. A brother, married like himself and having children, and two unmarried sisters, also lived with the old lady, and it is recorded that entire peace and harmony prevailed. Here the famous *Chaldee Manuscript* was concocted, amid such shouts of laughter, as Mrs. Gordon, the daughter and biographer of 'Christpher North' tells us, 'that the ladies in the room above sent to inquire in wonder what the gentlemen below were about' (see WILSON, pp. 87, 102).

At No. 52 SIR JAMES Y. SIMPSON, M.D., whose name will ever be associated with the introduction of the use of chloroform, lived from 1845 to his death. He is very vividly presented to us in the memoir in Chambers's *Biographical Dictionary*: 'He was a most genial companion, carrying the fresh playful feelings of boyhood into manhood. In his house and at his table there were always to be found men and women of all countries, classes, opinions, and pursuits; and, as has been tersely said, 'he literally did the honours of Edinburgh.' 'Sir James was not without his

faults, he was somewhat impulsive, vain, and quarrelsome
. . . . He had a striking personal appearance, though
somewhat lacking in refinement. In him, to quote the words
of Gerald Massey, the body of Bacchus was surmounted by
the head of Jove. His face and form, as they appeared in
earlier years, have been thus strikingly described; " A pale,
rather flattish face, massive bent brows, from under which
shone eyes, now piercing as it were to your inmost soul,
now melting with almost feminine tenderness; a coarsish
nose, with dilated nostrils; a finely chiselled mouth, which
seemed the most expressive feature of the face.' Mr. James
Payn says: 'I remember no one in his profession who im-
pressed me as being a man of genius more than he did. . . . .
The Doctor's own account of his first experiment with
chloroform is too good to be omitted : 'I had had the chloroform beside me for several days, but it seemed so unlikely
a liquid to produce results of any kind, that it was laid
aside; and on searching for another object among some
loose papers, after coming home very late one night, my
hand chanced to fall upon it; and I poured some of the
fluid into tumblers before my assistants, Dr. George Keith
and Dr. Duncan, and myself. Before sitting down to supper
we all inhaled the fluid, and were all under the mahogany
in a trice, to my wife's consternation and alarm.' Sir
James Simpson died in 1870, aged fifty-nine.

At No 13 the REV. SIR HENRY MONCREIFF WELLWOOD
lived many years. Sir Henry Moncreiff, to use the name by
which he was best known, was, says Lord Cockburn, 'one
of the most remarkable and admirable men of his age.
Small grey eyes, an aquiline nose, vigorous lips, a noble head,
and the air of a plain hereditary gentleman marked the outward man. The prominent qualities of his mind were strong
integrity and nervous sense. There never was a sounder un-
derstanding' (*Life of Jeffrey*). In his *Memorials of My Time*
Cockburn says: 'The Sunday suppers of Henry Moncreiff
are worthy of record. This most admirable and somewhat
old-fashioned gentleman was one of those who always dined
between sermons, probably without touching wine. He then
walked back—look at him—from his small house in the east
end of Queen Street to his church, with his bands, his little
cocked hat, his tall cane, and his cardinal air ; preached, if it
was his turn, a sensible practical sermon; walked home in the
same style, took tea about five, spent some hours in his study;
at nine had family prayers, at which he was delighted to see
the friends of his sons, after which the whole party sat down

E

to roasted hares, goblets of wine, and his powerful talk.'
Moncreiff died in 1827, at the age of seventy-two.

NORTH ST. DAVID STREET.

No. 6 has a painful though strong interest as associated with

6 NORTH ST. DAVID STREET.

the fallen fortunes of SIR WAL-
TER SCOTT. Here he came to
lodge with a Mrs. Brown, after
the break up of his home at
North Castle Street and the
death of his wife. In visiting
the house in North Castle
Street we quoted Captain Basil
Hall's account of his visit to
the deserted mansion, and how
he proceeded to call on his
friend at North St. David
Street. He proceeds: 'I was
rather glad to recognise my
old friend the Abbotsford but-
ler, who answered the door
. . . . At the top of the stairs
we saw a small tray, with a
single plate and glasses for
a solitary person's dinner. . . . As he rose to receive
us, he closed the volume which he had been extracting
from, and came forward to shake hands. He was, of
course, in deep mourning, with weepers, and the other
trappings of woe, but his countenance, though certainly a
little woe-begone was not cut into any very deep furrows
. . . . After sitting a quarter of an hour we came away, well
pleased to see our friend quite unbroken in spirit, and
though bowed down a little by the blast, and here and there
a branch the less, as sturdy in the trunk as ever.'   Scott's
entry in his *Journal* on May 12th, 1826, in this connection is too
interesting to be omitted: 'Edinburgh, Mrs. Brown's lodging,
North St. David Street.   May 12th. . . . . Well, here I am,
in Arden.   And I may say with Touchstone, "When I was at
home I was in a better place."   I must, when there is occasion,
draw to my own Bailie Nicol Jarvie's consolation; "one cannot carry the comforts of the Saut Market about with one."
Were I at ease in my mind, I think the body is very well
cared for.   Only one other lodger in the house, a Mr. Shandy
—a clergyman; and, despite his name, said to be a quiet
one' (see SCOTT, SIR WALTER, pp. 33, 56, 58, 74, 75).

At No. **9** SIR DAVID BREWSTER was living in 1808, at the time of his commencement of the *Encyclopædia* which bears his name, and which is said to have originated in a casual hint from two clerical friends, whom he met in Princes Street, of the need of a good and thorough work of the kind. He commenced his career in the ministry in 1807, but the failure to secure the living of Sprouston in 1809 appears to have led him to relinquish it. 'He felt himself free to follow the career so manifestly opening before him. Many said, however, that by so doing he was "blasting his prospects for life"' (*Home Life of Sir David Brewster*, by Mrs. M. M. Gordon). Brewster was born 1781 : died 1868 (see BREWSTER, p. 79).

In a line with Queen Street is

YORK PLACE.

No. **19** was the residence for many years before his death, which took place here, of DR. JOHN ABERCROMBIE, the eminent physician, and the author of *The Intellectual Powers*, ten editions of which were called for in as many years ; a result said to be partly attributable to 'the numerous cases set forth of peculiar mental phenomena, whose detailed records made a dry subject easy and entertaining reading'; the work having now no philosophical value. Lord Cockburn, indeed, said that Dr. Abercrombie's ' fame would perhaps have stood higher had he published fewer books.' His benevolence led him to give much of his time to attendance on the poor, and, to supplement his own. exertions, he appointed several of his student pupils to special districts, himself exercising a supervision of the whole. His death was the result of the bursting of a coronary artery—a somewhat exceptional disease of the heart—and occurred in his study after breakfast, whither he had retired before attending to the numerous patients who were waiting, his carriage standing ready at the door. His servant, thinking he was remaining there an unusual time, after the lapse of an hour entered and found him lifeless on the floor. He was an eminently pious man, and much esteemed in private life. He was sixty-three at the time of his death in 1844.

No. **32,** before 1820, seems from the Edinburgh Directory to have been numbered 34, as its occupant was the same. This was SIR HENRY RAEBURN, the artist, whose brush has portrayed almost all the celebrities of his time. 'In 1795,' it is stated in Anderson's *Scottish Nation*, 'he built a large house in York Place, the upper part of which was lighted from the roof, and fitted up as a gallery for exhibition'; while

the lower rooms were divided into convenient painting rooms. His dwelling-house was at St. Bernard's—a villa then distant from Edinburgh, but now within its limits. It is said that the suburb which has been built upon his property, commenced in his life-time, owes the elegance displayed in its general arrangement and details to his design. The story of Raeburn's marriage is a romantic one as told by Cunningham. 'One day a young lady presented herself at his studio, and desired to sit for her portrait. He instantly remembered having seen her in

32 YORK PLACE.

some of his excursions, when, with his sketch-book in his hand, he was noting down some fine stretches of scenery; and as the appearance of anything living and lovely gives an additional charm to a landscape, the painter, like Gainsborough in similar circumstances, had readily admitted her into his drawing. This circumstance, he said, had had its influence. On further acquaintance he found that, besides personal charms, she had sensibility and wit. His respect for her did not affect his skill of hand, but rather inspired it, and he succeeded in making a fine portrait. The lady . . . was much pleased with the skill and likewise with the manner of the artist; and, about a month or so after the adventure of the studio, she gave him her hand in marriage, bestowing at once an affectionate wife and a handsome fortune.' Raeburn died in 1823, aged 67.

No 47 was the residence of ALEXANDER NASMYTH, the father of the Scottish school of landscape painting, who also turned to a source of profit his taste in the improvement of the pleasure grounds of the wealthy and noble as a sort of professional adviser. It is said, also, that many of his suggestions for the improvement of the street architecture of Edinburgh were adopted. 'The capabilities, in an artistic point of view, of his native city, was the favourite theme of his evening conversations to the close of his long-protracted life; and many can still remember how ancient Athens itself was eclipsed by the pictures which he drew of what Edinburgh might be made through the advantages of her situation and the taste of her citizens' (Chambers's *Biographical Dictionary*). He lived a placid, uneventful life, devoting much of his time to tuition in his own house, where he opened a school of painting, and numbered his own large family of sons (one of whom—Patrick—afterwards became a successful artist) and daughters among his pupils. Born 1758; died 1840.

PICARDY PLACE.

At No. **16**, now a paper-hanger's shop, for many years before his death, which took place here, lived JOHN CLERK (LORD ELDIN), made Lord of Session in 1823. Carlyle, writing of his first arrival in Edinburgh, in 1809, says: 'The only figure I distinctly recollect and got printed on my brain that night was John Clerk, there irritably hitching about,' and remarks on his 'grim, strong countenance, with its black, far-projecting brows.' Lockhart, in *Peter's Letters to his Kinsfolk*, writes: 'This Mr. Clerk is unquestionably at the present time the greatest man among those who derive their chief fame from their appearance at the Scottish Bar. His face and figure attracted my particular attention, before I had the least knowledge of his name, or suspicion of his surpassing celebrity.' Going on to describe 'the features in themselves as good,' he says: 'How the habits of the mind have stamped their traces upon every part of the face; what sharpness, what razor-like sharpness, has indented itself about the wrinkles of his eyelids; the eyes themselves so quick, so grey, such bafflers of scrutiny.' Lord Brougham, in his *Autobiography*, says: 'John Clerk's intimacy was very close with the Principal [Robertson] and his sister, who both had great confidence in his practical sense upon most subjects, when not perverted by odd prejudices and fancies. For instance, she being, like him, a warm advocate of exercise as a means above everything of promoting health, used to quote him as saying, when asked "What were you to do in bad weather?" "Why, run up and down stairs; there is no better exercise, or better fitted to bring all the muscles into play."' Clerk was very lame, and quite indifferent to his appearance in the matter of dress,

It is related that when walking down High Street one day from the Court of Session, he overheard a young lady saying to her companion rather loudly, 'There goes Johnnie Clerk, the lame lawyer,' upon which he turned round and said, 'No, madam, I may be a lame man, but not a lame lawyer.' He was a great collector of pictures and prints, also of domestic animals. Lockhart says he had 'a stock of dogs that would serve to keep the whole population of a Mahometan city in disgust; and a perfect menagerie of the *genus felinum*. If one goes to consult him in his own chambers, I am told he is usually to be found sitting with a huge black tom cat on his shoulders . . . and surrounded in every direction with familiars of the same species.' Lord Eldin died in 1832, aged seventy-five. At the sale of his collection of paintings and prints, which took place here, the floor of the drawing-room gave way, and eighty or more persons, one of whom was killed, were precipitated into the room below, to the destruction also of much valuable china and numerous articles of vertu there displayed.

Opposite the end of Picardy Place, in Leith Walk, and a continuation of Greenside Place, is

BAXTER'S PLACE.

At No. 1, the lower portion of which is now built out as a large drapery establishment, resided ROBERT STEVENSON, the famous engineer, to whose talents is due the construction of the Bell Rock Lighthouse; the story of his experience in connection with which is one of physical discomfort and peril almost inconceivable; and steadfastly and bravely endured. He is said to have been highly estimable in private life, religious without ostentation, of a lively intelligence, and full of kindness and active benevolence. He died here in 1850, at the age of seventy-eight.

Returning southward along Leith Walk we pass up Little King Street—of which it may be truthfully said, that though short, a 'little goes a long way'; as the term 'up' is no figure of speech—by the side of the Theatre-Royal, to

ST. JAMES'S SQUARE.

At No. 31, still unchanged, ROBERT BURNS lived with Mr. William Cruikshank, one of the teachers in the High School, after his residence with Nicol in 1787. In his *Life of Burns*, Robert Chambers says : 'The house was composed of the two upper rooms of a lofty building in an airy situation in the New Town—then marked No. 2, now 30 St. James's Square. The poet's room had a window overlooking the green behind the Register House, as well as the Street entering the square. It was by far the most agreeable place in which he had ever had more than the most temporary lodging.' While here he made the acquaintance of his celebrated 'Clarinda,' Mrs. M'Lehose—'a lady,' writes Chambers, 'of exactly his own age, who, having been unhappily married to a man devoid of humanity and just moral feeling, was obliged to live separately from him in obscurity while bringing up her young family . . . of a somewhat voluptuous style of beauty, of lively and easy manners, of a poetical fabric of mind, with some wit, and

30 ST. JAMES'S SQUARE.

not too great a degree of refinement or delicacy.' On December 12th, Burns writes to her: 'I am here under the care of a surgeon, with a bruised limb extended on a cushion; and the tints of my mind vying with the livid horror preceding a midnight thunderstorm. A drunken coachman was the cause of the first, and incomparably the lightest evil: misfortune, bodily constitution, hell, and myself have formed a "quadruple alliance" to guarantee the other.' On January 21st he writes of 'six weeks' confinement,' and 'beginning to walk across the room,' but in the interim had paid several visits to the lady and to Miss Overend, at whose house he first met her. On one occasion he writes: 'I am certain I saw you, Clarinda,' [she had promised to fulfil her promise of giving him a nod at his window] 'but you don't look to the proper story for a poet's lodging, "where speculation roosted near the sky." I could almost have thrown myself over for very vexation. Why did not you look higher? It has spoiled my peace for this day.' In her next letter Clarinda laments her inability to discover the poet's window. On February 18th he left Edinburgh. Mr. Lawrence Hutton (*Literary Landmarks of Edinburgh*), states "on the authority of an old resident of St. James's Square to whom Clarinda had pointed it out herself," that it "was the topmost or attic windows in the gable looking towards the General Post Office in Waterloo Place " (see BURNS, p. 7).

At No. 4 died DAVID MARTIN, the artist, whose works are to be seen in Surgeons' Hall, the Advocates' Library, and Heriot's Hospital, and who has the credit of having produced the best portrait of Franklin. Raeburn was his pupil. He died in 1797, at the age of sixty-one. The premises are now used as a printing office, and for other business purposes.

ROUTE IV.

OUR starting-point is opposite the Caledonian Railway Station at the western end of Princes Street, and the present excursion includes the later and more handsomely built portion of the New Town.

RUTLAND STREET.

No. 23 is memorable as the residence, from about 1850 to the time of his death, of the genial author of *Rab and his Friends*, DR. JOHN BROWN, respecting whom, in the *Dictionary of National Biography*, we have the personal testimony of Mr. J. Taylor Brown: 'In his medical capacity he was remarkable for his close and accurate observations of symptoms, and constant attention to his patients. . . . He was first of all a physician, thoroughly devoted to his profession. . . . Few men in life have been more generally beloved. . . . In society he was natural and unaffected, with pleasantry and humour ever at com-

23 RUTLAND STREET.

mand; yet no one could suspect any tinge of frivolity in his character. With all the tenderness of a woman, he had a powerful, manly intellect, was full of practical sense, tact, and sagacity, and found himself perfectly at home with all men of the best minds of his time who happened to come across him. Lord Jeffrey, Lord Cockburn, Mr. Thackeray, Mr. Ruskin, Sir Henry Taylor, were all happy to number themselves among his most attached friends.' The first series of his *Horæ Subsecivæ*, which included *Rab and his Friends* was produced during his residence here in 1858-9. He died in 1882, at the age of seventy-two (see BROWN, p. 98).

Returning to the corner of Princes Street, we pass down

EAST MAITLAND STREET,

formerly consisting of private houses. No. **6** Shandwick Place, on the north side of the street, stands on the site of the last residence of SIR WALTER SCOTT in Edinburgh. Hogg writes in *Domestic Manners and Private Life of Scott*: 'The last time Margaret saw him was at his own house in Maitland Street, a very short time before he finally left it. We were passing from Charlotte Square. . . . I said: "See, yon is Sir Walter's house, at yon red lamp."' It was here that on the 15th of February 1830, he was stricken with paralysis after his return at two o'clock in the afternoon from the Parliament House. Alarming symptoms during an interview in his library with Miss Young of Hawick, whose memoirs of her father he had undertaken to revise, compelled him to shorten the interview. Lockhart says: 'He got up and staggered to the drawing-room, where Anne Scott and my sister, Violet Lockhart, were sitting. They rushed to meet him, but he fell at all his length on the floor ere they could reach him. He remained speechless for about ten minutes, by which time a surgeon had arrived and bled him. He was cupped again in the evening, and gradually recovered possession of speech, and of all his faculties, in so far that, the occurrence being kept quiet, when he appeared abroad again after a short interval, people in general observed no serious change (see SCOTT, pp. 33, 56, 58, 66, 75).

At No. **23** Maitland Street, now a shop, JOHN GIBSON LOCKHART was living in 1819-20. This was about the time that he wrote *Peter's Letters to his Kinsfolk*, under the pseudonym of Peter Morris—a vivid series of portraits of contemporary celebrities, of which free use has been made in this work. In 1816 he had qualified to practise as a barrister ; 'but,' says a writer in Chamber's *Biographical Dictionary*, 'it was soon evident that he was not to win fame or fortune as an advocate.' He lacked, indeed, that power without which all legal attainments are useless to a barrister. He could not make a speech. Accordingly, when he rose to speak on a case, his first sentences were only a plunge into the mud ; while all that followed was but a struggle to get out of it. . . . He became a briefless barrister, and paced the boards of Parliament House, discussing with his equally luckless brethren the passing questions of politics and literary criticism. He made a happy allusion to this strange professional infirmity at a dinner which was given by his friends in Edinburgh, on his departure to assume the charge of the *Quarterly Review*. He attempted to address them, and broke down as usual; but covered his retreat with, 'Gentlemen, you know that if I could speak, we would not have been here.' Lockhart married Scott's eldest daughter in 1820 (see LOCKHART, p. 91). Born 1794; died 1854.

Passing partly round Coates Crescent, we enter

WALKER STREET.

No. **3** was occupied by SIR WALTER SCOTT and his daughter on his return from the continent at the close of 1830. He is described as working very hard here at his *Life of Napoleon*, and suffering much from rheumatism, contracted from a damp bed in a French inn; and walking, when he could walk at all, to and from Parliament House, through the Princes Street Gardens (see SCOTT, pp. 33, 56, 58, 66, 74).

Opposite to Coates Crescent is

ATHOLL CRESCENT.

At No. **16** lived ROBERT CADELL, the publisher of Scott's later works, formerly partner with Constable, his father-in-law, and of whom Scott writes in his *Journal*: 'Constable without Cadell is like getting the clock without the pendulum; the one having the ingenuity, the other the caution of the business.' Cadell, after the failure of Constable, and dissolution of the partnership, joined Scott in purchasing the copyright of the novels from *Waverley* to *Quentin Durward* for £8500; and by publishing the immensely successful 'Author's Edition,' Scott relieved himself of a great part of his liabilities. The house is above all interesting from the fact that Scott stayed here on one occasion. Lockhart says: 'On the 31st of January [1831], Miss Scott being too unwell for a journey, Sir Walter went alone to Edinburgh for the purpose of executing his last will. He (for the first time in his native town) took up his quarters at a hotel, but the noise of the street disturbed him during the night . . . and next day he was persuaded to remove to his bookseller's house in Atholl Crescent. In the apartment allotted to him there, he found several little pieces of furniture which some kind person had purchased for him at the sale in Castle Street, and which he presented to Mrs. Cadell.' He writes to Lockhart: 'Here I saw various things that belonged to poor No. 39. I had many sad thoughts on seeing and handling them—but they are in kind keeping, and I was glad they had not gone to strangers.' Lockhart describes Cadell as 'a cool, inflexible specimen of the national character.' He had 'a handsome estate in land and considerable landed property' at the time of his death, which took place at Ratho House, Midlothian, from which he was driven to his business house in St. Andrew Square every morning at nine o'clock, so punctually that the inhabitants on the line of route knew the time by 'the Ratho coach.' His death occurred in 1849, in his sixty-second year.

At the southern end of Atholl Crescent is

MANOR PLACE.

At No. **3**, formerly No. 2—the numbers were altered in 1882 —Lord Cockburn lived 'in chambers' when in town until his death at Bonaly in 1854 (see COCKBURN, p. 60).

At No. **21**, formerly No 11, SIR WILLIAM HAMILTON lived 1829-39. Veitch, his biographer, describes it as 'a sunny

pleasant row of houses then, at the extreme west end of Edinburgh, which looked into the grounds of the old manor house of Coates, and afforded easy access to the country.' On his country walks, we are told, 'he liked to have a companion, but the conversation was usually rather scanty, at least on his part—the train of thought in which he had been engaged continuing apparently to occupy him. The truth is, it was rather his way when on a walk with the more intimate of his friends, to set them off on their respective hobbies—it might be genealogy or mesmerism—while he himself, though putting in his word now and then, followed the bent of his own thoughts.

MANOR PLACE.

He would then be seen walking considerably in advance, on the opposite side of the road from his companion— perhaps repeating aloud to himself some Greek, Latin, or English verses, quite unconscious of what he was sounding forth. Some lady friends, who often met Sir William and his companions returning in this fashion from their stroll, would, naturally enough, ask whether the two had had a quarrel.' Mr. Hamilton Gray, quoted by Veitch, describes Sir William as 'tall of stature and strongly built, with a large noble-looking head, a firm mouth, and magnificent black eyes. His brow was heavy and massive, producing upon me something of the same effect as Sir Walter Scott's when perfectly quiet. His mouth, too, had a little touch of satire and severity about it which somehow held me in awe ; but all the severity and all the heaviness vanished when once he began to speak, dispelled by the fire of his eye and the kindness of his smile. Sir William's language was fluent, his manner energetic, and his humour versatile.' Sir William Hamilton removed to Manor Place from Great King Street on his marriage to an estimable lady, who 'added to her ordinary duties nearly the constant work of amanuensis to her husband.' On leaving here he returned to Great King Street in 1839 (see HAMILTON, pp. 89, 94).

At No. 25, formerly No. 13, William Chambers was living in 1862 (see CHAMBERS, post).

Crossing Manor Place at its northern end is

CHESTER STREET.

No. 25 was the residence of WILLIAM CHAMBERS at the time when he was Lord Provost of Edinburgh 1867-70. The following description of one whose appearance is still fresh in the memories of many of his fellow-citizens, is from the *Dictionary of National Biography*: 'About the middle height, dark in feature, with hair that comparatively early became grey: somewhat reserved in manner, he was not popular with those who knew him slightly. . . . He had no special literary faculty, but his writings exhibit strong common sense, and he knew how to make a subject interesting. It is, however, not as the popular writer or successful publisher, but as the good citizen, that he will be longest remembered. The name of William Chambers will always be connected with the city of Edinburgh which he beautified, and the Church of St. Giles which he restored.' An 'amiable weakness' of William Chambers, according to Mr. James Payn (*Some Literary Recollections*), appears to have been a too great partiality for referring to the days of his early struggles, and the time when he earned his matutinal hot roll by reading *Roderick Random* to the baker and his men before dawn, 'seated on a folded-up sack in the sill of the window with a book in one hand, and a penny candle stuck in a bottle in the other: reminiscences which his brother Robert did his best to discourage.' He died three days before the re-opening of St. Giles's Church—on the restoration of which he had expended between twenty and thirty thousand pounds—living to the age of eighty-three, with a constitution unimpaired by the privations of his youth, and the retention to the last, according to Mr. Payn, of a habit of 'bolting' his food—'a relic, doubtless, of the time when he worked sixteen hours a day, and allowed himself a quarter of an hour for his meals.' He was born with the century, and died in 1883.

We return, by Manor Place, to

MELVILLE STREET.

No. 45 was the residence, from about 1840 to 1853 (his name disappears from the *Edinburgh Directory* after the latter year), of GEORGE COMBE, the phrenologist. Though giving much of his time to lecturing and writing on his favourite so-called science, he was devoted to his profession as a Writer to the Signet, and took also an active part in public life. He married a daughter of Mrs. Siddons, who survived him. He was a man of delicate constitution, but by regular living and temperate habits contrived to live out the allotted time of three score and ten. His collection of books on phrenology is now in the Advocates' Library. Born 1788; died 1858.

No. 29 was the residence of the REV. ANDREW THOMSON D.D., 'the most popular preacher of the time in Edinburgh, occupying a new and magnificent place of worship in the finest square and most fashionable neighbourhood in the whole city': so wrote Lockhart, in *Peter's Letters*. Then he proceeds: 'Mr. Andrew Thomson is a much younger man than those I have described [Sir Henry Moncreiff and Dr. Inglis], and perhaps his talents are still better adapted than those of either for producing a powerful impression on the minds of people living in what may be called strictly the society of Edinburgh .... I am assured that church-going

was a thing completely out of fashion among the fine folks of
the New Town of Edinburgh till this man was removed from
a church he formerly held in
the Old Town, and established
under the splendid dome of
St. George's. . . . . He is an
active and muscular man,
about forty, and carries in his
countenance the stamp of a
nature deficient in none of
those elements which are most
efficient in giving a man com-
mand over the minds of persons placed under the constant
operation of his intellect.
Most of his features, indeed,
are rather homely than otherwise in their conformation—
but they are all well-defined,
massy, and full of power. His
eyes are quick, and firmly set

29 MELVILLE STREET.

—his lips are bold, and nervous in their motions no less
than in their quiescence—his nose is well carved, and
joins firmly with a forehead of unquestionably very fine
and commanding structure.' Dr. Thomson, apart from his
celebrity as a preacher, appears to have enjoyed the esteem
of his contemporaries as a liberal-minded non-sectarian
—holding out the hand of fellowship to all descriptions of
dissenters ; active in the discharge of all his ministerial
duties ; energetic in behalf of the freedom of the slave. His
printed lectures, sermons, and addresses fill many volumes.
Dr. Guthrie, in his *Autobiography*, remarking respecting Dr.
Blair that he was extremely fastidious in his selection of
those who should fill his pulpit in his absence, says : ' He was
not so easy about supplying his pulpit as Dr. Andrew
Thomson. Some one complaining to the latter of the poor
substitutes he set up to preach in his absence, said : "You put
everybody into your pulpit, Dr. Thomson"; "No, no," replied
the ready-witted Andrew, "though I believe I put any-
body."' Dr. Thomson died suddenly, falling on the threshold
of his house which he was entering, in 1831, being only fifty-
two years of age.

No. 1 was the residence for some years prior to 1827 of SIR
DAVID BREWSTER. In the *Home Life of Sir David Brewster*
some interesting traits of his character are well described :

'He used the strongest language to express what to other minds would have been a comparatively small trial or event —the smallest circumstances connected with food, servants, visits, journeys, or such like, were created by a naturally irritable temper and finely strung nerves into serious events, and, if the slightest thing went wrong, were commented upon in terms so distressed as would have led a stranger to believe that some calamity of unusual magnitude had occurred. . . . His power of telling sarcasm was very great—it was a weapon which he too much delighted to use, and which came too easily to his hand when he wielded a pen : his entire freedom from it in daily life and speech was, however, remarkable.' The following is told in illustration of his singular timidity. 'At the time Lord Rosse's telescope was drawing so many scientific men across the Channel, he was asked if he were going too: "Oh no!" he said, "he was too much afraid of the sea." My father tried to represent to him what a simple matter it was; he thought nothing of it himself: he just went straight to bed on going on board, and awoke on arriving at his destination. Sir David exclaimed in unaffected horror, "What! go to your naked bed" (a Scottish expression for going really to bed) "in the middle of the ocean." Another story somewhat betrayed the philosopher's want of self-control : he was talking of a severe fit of toothache he had had, and my father asked him, "What did you do?" (meaning, what remedy had he applied)—"Do!" said Sir David, "I just sat and *roared*!"' Brewster died in 1868, having attained the great age of eighty-seven (see BREWSTER, p. 67).

Nearly opposite to Melville Street is the south side of

RANDOLPH CRESCENT.

At No. 3 lived JOHN BLACKWOOD, whose function as editor of *Blackwood's Magazine*, subsequent to the death of his elder brother in 1845, was anticipated at school, where his display of literary tastes procured for him the nickname of 'The Little Editor.' Hospitable and convivial in his tastes, his house in Edinburgh, and his country place at St. Andrews, were the frequent recipients as guests of the authors with whom he had business relations. 'He will be a heavy loss to me,' wrote George Eliot; 'he has been bound up with what I most cared for in my life for more than twenty years; and his good qualities have made many things easy to me that, without him, would often have been difficult.' To John Blackwood, in fact, is due the credit of prompt recognition of the genius of George Eliot, whose

Scenes of Clerical Life, sent to him anonymously, first appeared in his *Magazine*. £5000 was paid by him for one of her later works. He died in 1879, aged sixty-one.

In the centre of Randolph Crescent we enter

GREAT STUART STREET,

To No. 16 WILLIAM EDMONDSTOUNE AYTOUN removed from Inverleith Terrace in 1853. Colonel Hamley, quoted in the *Life* by Sir Theodore Martin, found him at this time, 'sober in gait, slow and gentle in voice, and with a student-like stoop in his shoulders,' advancing, 'as shyly as a young girl. . . . . At this time he must have lost a good deal of the robust health and elasticity of spirits of his earlier days. He did not look more than his age, his colour was still fresh, and his brown hair was neither thinned nor silvered, but he was extremely indisposed to exertion.' In referring to his intended removal here, he writes: 'Last week I purchased a house in Great

GREAT STUART STREET.

Stuart Street, big enough to lodge a patriarch. I am not frightened at what I have done: I am simply stupefied. There will be plumbers, and the gas-fitters, and the painters; hum of upholstery work, and the slave that vendeth carpets, with all manner of minor harpies upon me at once. . . . . I have just been walking about the house after the manner of Solomon Eagle, with a brazier on my head, exclaiming, "Woe! woe!" to the terror of the housemaid.' Aytoun died in 1865, aged fifty-two (see AYTOUN, pp. 96, 106).

AINSLIE PLACE.

At No. 23 DEAN RAMSAY was living from 1865. In 1824 he was Curate of St. George's Chapel, York Place, and two years later of St. Paul's, Carrubber's Close: 'The sermons I then got credit for,' he wrote in 1843, 'we should all think little of now.' He married when curate of St. John's in 1829, and in 1846 became Dean of the Diocese of Edinburgh.

In a letter written here, March 14th 1865, congratulating himself on three thousand copies of the 'People's Edition' of the *Reminiscences* having been sold in the first week, he writes: 'I have been thirty-seven years in St. John's, and only met with kindness and respect. I have done much for my church, and that is acknowledged by every one . . . . But I don't expect to hold on much longer; I feel changed, and at times not equal to much exertion.' He was then seventy-two. In the year of his death he wrote: 'I am preparing for a twenty-second edition of the *Reminis-*

23 AINSLIE PLACE.

cences. Who would have thought it? No man.' Of this delightful book Cosmo Innes, in the biography prefixed to the later editions, says: 'While there were so many things to endear it to the peasantry of Scotland, it was not admired by them alone . . . . Dickens, Guthrie, ... Bishop Wordsworth, Dean Stanley, how eagerly they received the simple stories of Scotland told without ornament.' The same writer says of him: 'The High Churchman may think him unduly careless about forms and ceremonies; but, loving him very well, I yet wish to represent the Dean as he really was; above all things full of charity, loving religion as he understood the religion of the gospel, and not much concerned, not really deeply concerned, about the shape and dress in which it presented itself.' The Dean was an accomplished flute player, passionately fond of Handel's music. In the appendix to Cosmo Innes's memoir Lauderdale Burnett writes: 'How accomplished he was! what knowledge he had on many subjects; his fine taste, his gentleness, and Christian piety; how amusing he was, and such droll things broke out every now and then! even to the last so genial and social, and altogether such a man that we "ne'er shall look upon his like again!"' He died in 1872, aged seventy nine.

On the left hand, or west side of Ainslie Place,

No. 6 was the home, from 1836 until the time of his death, of SIR CHARLES BELL, the eminent surgeon, and discoverer

of the distinct functions of the nerves. His life, for the
most part, was spent in London, where he commenced to
practise his profession in 1805. He became a member of the
Royal College of Surgeons in 1813, and his examination was
limited as reported by himself, to a question as to what
disease in his opinion Buonoparte would die of. Of his great
discovery, Lady Bell writes: 'I must recall one memorable
evening. We had a cottage at Hampstead. He drove to
Haverstock Hill, and walked on. He came in breathless, and
sat down, saying, "O May! I have discovered what will im-
mortalise me." He placed a sheet of paper on the table, and
sketched on it what he afterwards called *The Classification
of the Nerves*.' This was in 1827. On his appointment to the
Professorship of Surgery in the University of Edinburgh,
and in the bustle of packing up before leaving London, he
wrote: 'Until I build up a corner in Ainslie Place, and
see familiar things about me, I shall be like a bird whose
nest is a boy's hat.' Lady Bell says: 'We came to Scotland
at the right season, and were welcomed by all whom we
wished to welcome us. . . . The windows of Ainslie Place
looked to the glorious colouring of the north-west skies,
to Corstorphine Hills, and the distant Grampians. The
garden was in terraces, down to the Water of Leith, and
the walks there among the sweet-briar hedges made our
home in Edinburgh very delightful.' Sir Charles writes
to John Richardson: 'This is a capital house, with two
spare rooms, and all your old friends within a gunshot,
and all living in harmony and kindness. London is a cold
place—people do not meet as if they wished and meant to
live together. It is only in county relationship what I
mean, and what you may have here.' Later on he writes:
'I am busy from morning till night—never without object
or employment, but nothing to tell you of . . . unless it be
our evenings: Marie reading to me while I sketch for
lecture.' Lady Bell says of him that he was 'methodical,
and never in a hurry.' 'He was modest, and did not speak
much, but there was raciness and originality in his talk.'
'His manner of composing was unequal. At times he
seemed inspired, and as if the thoughts rushed too rapidly
for expression. At others he seemed labouring. And then
we stopped. He took up his pencils or modelling or etching
tools, and listened to reading.' Like Darwin, Bell loved
a novel for relaxation, and on the same condition—that
it 'ended well.' The above extracts are taken from *The
Life and Letters of Sir Charles Bell*. He appears to have
been universally beloved. Lord Cockburn (*Memorials of My*

Time) says: 'If ever I knew a generally and practically happy man, it was Sir Charles Bell'; and Jeffrey writes of him as 'good, kind-hearted, happy Charlie Bell'; while he himself said: 'There is not a man in my profession with whom I am not good friends.' He died of angina pectoris, while on a visit near Worcester, in 1842, at the age of sixty-eight.

At No. 5, the house of a friend whom he was visiting—not his *residence*, as stated by Grant in *Old and New Edinburgh*—DUGALD STEWART, who, since the death of his son in 1812, had retired to Kinneil House, near Bo'ness, died suddenly in the year 1828, at the age of seventy-five (see STEWART, page 23).

No. 3 was the residence of WILLIAM BLACKWOOD from about 1830 to the time of his death, which occurred in 1834; his age being fifty-eight (see BLACKWOOD, pp. 47, 54, 111).

MORAY PLACE

follows a continuation of Great Stuart Street.

At No. 47, on the north side, died SIR JAMES WELLWOOD MONCREIFF, the eminent judge, and active Whig politician, who was a 'public character' of a sort and identified himself with Whig politics at the early age of sixteen; when the organisers of a meeting at the circus, 'being unaccustomed at that time to such assemblages,' having forgotten to provide illumination, and Henry Erskine having commenced his address in the dark, the young Moncreiff procured a tallow candle, and held it in front of the orator until a more abundant light was provided, The memoir in Chambers's *Biographical Dictionary* has the following: 'It was as a member of the General Assembly of the Church of Scotland that his great talents for investigation and debate, combined with his well-known integrity, were chiefly valued'; and quotes Lord Cockburn's eulogium: 'I am not aware how his moral nature could have been improved. A truer friend, a more upright judge, or a more affectionate man could not be.' Jeffrey called him 'The whole duty of man.' He died in 1851, at the age of seventy-five.

Retracing our steps past Great Stuart Street we reach

No. 24, where FRANCIS JEFFREY removed from George Street in 1817, and here he died. His connection with the

Edinburgh Review ended in 1829. In 1832 he was made Lord
of Session. His celebrity, however, is entirely that of the
editor and critic, not of the judge. It is curious to read
in his letters at eighteen: 'I feel I shall never be a great
man, unless it be as a poet'; and, 'whence arises my
affection for the moon? I do not believe there is a being,
of whatever denomination, upon whom she lifts the light
of her countenance, who is so glad to see her as I am.'
His residence here, alternating with visits to his country
house at Craigcrook, two miles from Edinburgh, was
spent in the enjoyment of comparative leisure. One autumn
day in 1849, he took what he felt to be a farewell view of
the beauties of his suburban retreat, and 'on January 22d,
after a brisk walk round the Calton Hill, he was attacked
by bronchitis, a complaint to which for several years he had
been more or less subject . . . and after four days' illness
in which he suffered little, and anticipated a speedy
recovery, he breathed his last on the 26th instant. He,
too, felt the ruling passion strong in death, for in his dreams
during the three nights prior to his dissolution, the spirit
of the Edinburgh Reviewer predominated, so that he was
examining proof sheets, reading newspapers, and passing
judgment upon arguments or events as they rose before
his mind's eye, in the most fantastical variety.' His wife
survived him only a few months. He was seventy-seven
years old at his death (see JEFFREY, pp. 32, 42, 55, 63, 105).

THOMAS CARLYLE was a temporary resident here with
Mrs. Carlyle, in 1828, after leaving Comely Bank. He
writes: 'The flitting to Craigenputtock took place in May.
We stayed a week in Moray Place (Jeffrey's fine new house
there) after our furniture was on the road' (*Reminiscences*).
(See CARLYLE, pp. 100, 103.)
A little further on, leading out of Moray Place

DOUNE TERRACE.

At No. 1, in the later years of his life, lived ROBERT
CHAMBERS, one of the firm of publishers, and still more
memorable as the accomplished and industrious author
and compiler of many admirable works, including *The
Dictionary of Eminent Scotsmen*, of which liberal use has
been made in these pages. In the *Memoirs of William and
Robert Chambers* [1884], we read that 'Visitors from all parts
of the world were at all times welcome at No. 1 Doune
Terrace, and with these might be seen commingled some of

the most notable men of the time—Lord Jeffrey, Lord Cockburn, Christopher North, Lockhart, the Ettrick Shepherd,
De Quincey, Dr. Moir ("Delta"), Professor Aytoun, George
and Andrew Combe, Lord Ivory, Sir Adam Ferguson, . . .
besides many noted Edinburgh wits and conversationalists
who "had their day," and, as is mostly the fate of such
ephemera, have "ceased to be."' From the same source we
take the following description of the two brothers : ' William
was about the middle size, thin, muscular, and wiry ; Robert
slightly taller, and of a fuller and more sanguine habit.
Both were men of marked appearance, more especially the
younger ; and it was no uncommon thing for strangers to
turn and look after Robert Chambers in the street, certain
that he, unknown to them, was no ordinary individual. In
youth, William was dark in hair, Robert of a fairer type,
with brown hair ; but at quite an early period of their life
their hair was tinged with white, and became wholly or
nearly so before they had reached the age of fifty.' ' Robert,'
says the writer, 'was so constituted that remarkably little
sleep sufficed for him when in health, seldom more than five
hours out of the twenty-four being so spent.' Breakfast at
eight, writing in his own house until one, a visit to the
office, a walk of an hour or two and retirement to his study—
when not dining out or entertaining at home—to work from
eight till one, appears to have been his daily routine, and
when we find that early wakefulness in the morning, and
reading in bed for an hour or two, was also the rule, it is not
surprising to learn that close application and the consequent
confinement, at an advanced age, in the production of *The
Book of Days*, in London, was, to use his own words, his
' death blow ;' injuring his health to such an extent that he
never quite recovered it. Mr. James Payn, who edited
Chambers's Journal for many years, has some interesting
notes of our subject in his *Literary Recollections*: 'His
manner was dry, and though his eye wrinkled with humour,
I did not immediately recognise it as such . . . Robert
Chambers's humour was of the good-natured sort. His
nature was essentially "good"; from the pleasure he took in
the prosperity of his friends, I used to call him the " Well-
Wisher"; nor did he confine himself, as so many benevolent
folks do, to writing. I was in intimate communication with
him for twenty years, every one of which increased my
respect for him ; and when he died I lost one of the truest
friends I ever had. . . . His manner, however, on a first
acquaintance, was somewhat solid and unsympathetic. He
had a very striking face and figure . . . but a stranger would

have taken him for a divine, possibly even for one of the "unco' guid." In London, his white tie, and grave demeanour, caused him to be always taken for a clergyman; a very great mistake, which used to tickle him exceedingly. . . . He held two pews, each at different churches. I asked him why he had taken them in duplicate. "Because," he replied, "when I am not in the one it will always be concluded by the charitable that I am in the other." My friends, his daughters, were very lively and full of fun, and on one occasion, on their coming back to Edinburgh from some stay in London, their father was thus congratulated by an old church-goer on their return, "We were glad to see them back again," he said; "yours is such a merry pew."' Robert Chambers died in 1871, at the age of sixty-nine, at St. Andrews, whither he retired.

GLOUCESTER PLACE.

At No. 6, from about 1825 to his death, lived JOHN WILSON, the 'Christopher North' of *Blackwood's Magazine*. 'He was essentially a man of genius,' writes Sir Archibald Alison in his *Autobiography*: 'You could not converse with him five minutes without perceiving it. His very look revealed the fervour of his mind. Blue piercing eyes, thin and flying yellow hair, a fair complexion, and sanguine temperament, bespoke the Danish blood. . . . He never courted the great: while maintaining their cause with strenuous ability, he was never seen at their tables. . . . His heart contained many of the purest and noblest sentiments, but with these was combined a strange mixture of humorous drollery, sometimes not of the most refined kind,

6 GLOUCESTER PLACE.

which strongly appears in his *Miscellaneous Essays*. . . . He scarcely ever began to work till a day or two before the article required to be printed, and then he wrote straight on, often for sixteen or seventeen hours before leaving his room. In the intervening three or four weeks, till the periodical demand of the printer's devil returned, he did little or nothing, dreaming over poetry, fishing up the Tweed, or wandering in romantic rapture through the Highland glens.' Carlyle writes of him in 1827: 'A man of the most fervid temperament, fond of all stimulating things, from tragic poetry down to whisky punch. He snuffed, and smoked cigars, and drank liquors, and talked in a most indescribable style. . . . Daylight came on before we parted; indeed, it was towards three o'clock as the Professor and I walked home, smoking as we went. . . . He is a broad, sincere man of six feet, with long dishevelled hair, and two blue eyes, keen as an eagle's' (Froude's *Carlyle*). Lockhart in *Peter's Letters*, calls him, 'a very robust, athletic man, broad across the back, firm set upon his limbs, and having altogether very much of that sort of air which is inseparable from the consciousness of great bodily energies.' He died in 1854, at the age of sixty-nine (see WILSON, pp. 64, 102).

Turning to the right, the first turning on the left leads to

ROYAL CIRCUS.

To No. 21—close to the point of entrance on the right— ROBERT JAMESON, Regius Professor of Natural History, removed about 1820, and here he resided until his death. We give elsewhere some particulars of his career. From Chambers's *Biographical Dictionary* we learn that, 'although of slender body, his general health was good, and his wiry frame could endure much fatigue without injury; and his first tokens of decay were from repeated and severe attacks of bronchitis during the last two years of his life.' An extract from an unnamed biographer—whom we have been unable to identify—states that 'he had fine natural talents which had been carefully cultivated, and were applied with vigour to the studies in which he delighted. He was a careful observer, a comprehensive thinker, and his industry was unwearied. He was never satisfied with loose and general notions on any subject; his range of information was wide, and what he knew he knew thoroughly. He was practical and anxious to be useful, in days when science and practice stood apart as if they were two repellent forces. He did much towards neutralising these states; and was one of the pioneers to whom we are indebted for that union of science and practice which is now the prevailing feature of our time.' Jameson died in 1854, at the age of eighty-two (see JAMESON, p. 39).

The first turning out of Royal Circus leads to

HOWE STREET.

At No. **18**—now a wine merchant's—from about 1818 to
1827, SIR WILLIAM HAMILTON lived with his mother and
sisters. Carlyle writes in his *Journal*: 'Well onward in
my student life in Edinburgh, I think it may have been in
1819 or 1820 . . . somewhere in Gabriel's Road, there looked
out upon me from the Princes Street or St. David Street
side, a back window on the ground floor of a handsome
enough house; window which had no curtains; and visible
on the sill of it was a quantity of books lying about, gilt
quartos and conspicuous volumes, several of them; evidently
the sitting-room and working-room of a studious man, whose
lot, in this safe seclusion, I viewed with a certain loyal
respect. "Has a fine silent neighbourhood," thought I; "a
fine north light, and wishes to save it all." Inhabitant
within I never noticed by any other symptom, but from my
comrades soon learned whose house and place of study it
was.' On this passage, Veitch, Sir William Hamilton's
biographer, remarks: 'There is an inaccuracy here respecting the locality of the house. At this period Sir William
was living at Howe Street.' Carlyle, who afterwards came
to know him well, says: 'I recollect well the bright affable
manners of Sir William, radiant with frank kindness, honest
humanity, and intelligence ready to help; and how completely prepossessing they were. A fine firm figure of middle
height, one of the finest cheerfully-serious human faces, of
square, solid, and yet rather aquiline type . . . and a pair of
the beautifullest kindly-beaming eyes, well open, and every
now and then with a lambency of smiling fire in them.' 'So
exquisitely free was Sir William from all ostentation of
learning,' writes De Quincey, 'that unless the accidents of
conversation made a natural opening for display, such as
it would have been affectation to evade, you might have
failed altogether to suspect that an accomplished scholar
was present. . . . In general, my conviction was that I had
rarely seen a person who manifested less of self-esteem
under any of the forms by which it ordinarily reveals itself—
whether of pride or vanity, or full-blown arrogance, or heart-
chilling reserve.' Sir William removed from Howe Street,
on his mother's death in 1827, to Great King Street. Born in
1788, he died in 1856 (see HAMILTON, pp. 76, 94).

No. **11** was the residence of JOHN EWBANK, the marine
and landscape painter, 1830-31, at the time of his decline
(see EWBANK, p. 103).

Continuing along Howe Street we reach

HERIOT ROW.

No. 44 was the residence for many years, from 1814, of the
REV. ARCHIBALD ALISON, author of *Essays on Taste.* Lord

Cockburn (*Memorials of My Time*)
writes of him as 'the most distinguished of the Episcopal clergy
of Edinburgh, and, so far as I know,
of Scotland. A most excellent and
agreeable man ; richly imbued with
literature ; a great associate with
Dugald Stewart, Playfair, Dr.
Gregory, Jeffrey, and all the eminent among us ; delightful in society ;
and, in truth, without a single
defect except the amiable one of
too soft a manner.' We learn
from the *Autobiography* of his son,
Sir Archibald Alison, that 'he had
retired from his clerical duties ever
since a dreadful attack of inflamma-

44 HERIOT ROW.

tion of the lungs, which brought him to the verge of the grave
in 1830. That attack destroyed above half of the single lung
remaining after a prolonged illness in 1805. The remaining
nine years of his life were spent in retirement. . . . During
the winter he remained strictly confined to his house in
Edinburgh, repairing to his country residence in the summer,
and there he died.' His vision, it is said, was much impaired, 'the sight of one eye being nearly lost from the
effects of the dangerous but seductive habit of reading in
bed.' 'No man who held fierce and uncompromising opinions
on the principles of religion and morals looked with more
indulgence on the failings of others, or passed through the
world in more perfect charity and goodwill to all men. No
man who had lived much in society could retire with more
pleasure at all periods of life into domestic privacy, and into
the solitude of the country. . . . No man who had attained
a high reputation as a preacher and an author was ever
more indifferent to popular applause, as compared with
the consciousness of the performance of duty.' The picture presented by the contributor to the *Dictionary of
National Biography* is less attractive: 'He seems to
have led a studious, retired, and somewhat indolent life,
generally lying in bed "reading or thinking," until two

o'clock in the afternoon; he never wrote except under strong pressure, and his books are only fragments of a larger design.' His sermons, written in the polished style of Blair, were much admired; and his son says, 'as impressive pieces of pulpit eloquence they were excellent,' but too optimistic in their views of human nature. His father, he considered, 'had not enough of the devil in him to find the devil out.' He died in 1839, aged eighty-two.

SIR ARCHIBALD ALISON, the Historian, also resided here with his father until his marriage in 1825 (see ALISON, p. 61).

At No. **6** HENRY MACKENZIE, author of *The Man of Feeling*, resided in his later years. Lord Cockburn says of him: 'His excellent conversation, agreeable family, good evening parties, and the interest attached to united age and reputation made his house one of the pleasantest. . . . The title of "The Man of Feeling" adhered to him ever after the publication of that novel [in 1771]; and it was a good example of the difference there sometimes is between a man and his work. Strangers used to fancy that he must be a pensive sentimental Harley; whereas he was far better—a hard-headed practical man, as full of worldly wisdom as most of his fictitious characters are devoid of it; and this without in the least impairing the affectionate softness of his heart. In person he was thin, shrivelled, and yellow, kiln-dried; with something, when seen in profile, of the clever wicked look of Voltaire' (*Memorials of My Time*). His yellow kiln-dried aspect appears to have been no indication of lack of bodily vigour, as he lived until eighty-six, and was an active sportsman in his old age. He died in 1831 (see MACKENZIE, p. 26).

At No. **3** JAMES BALLANTYNE was living in 1823, having removed hither from St. John Street (see BALLANTYNE, pp. 17, 98).
Dundas Street, the next turning in Heriot Row, leads, northward to

NORTHUMBERLAND STREET,

No. **25,** to the right on the north side, was the residence in 1823-24 of JOHN GIBSON LOCKHART. He gives us his own portrait, writing in the character of Peter Morris: 'His features are regular, and quite definite in their outlines; his forehead is well-advanced, largest, I think, in the region of observation and perception. . . . Mr. Lockhart is a very young person, and I would hope may soon find that there are much better things in literature than satire, let it be as good-humoured as you will.' Sir Archibald Alison says of him in his *Autobiography*: 'His hair was dark, his eye keen, his lips thin, his complexion sallow, his manners polished but reserved. In general society he was silent and observant; in his intimate circle joyous and expansive.' In another place he says that Lockhart's satirical turn 'made him a most amusing companion, but at the same time, mingled a certain feeling of distrust, even with the affection of his most intimate friends; for you never could tell how soon you yourself might become the object of the shafts which he launched with so unmerciful a hand at others.' In 1825 Lockhart went to London as editor of the *Quarterly Review* (see LOCKHART, p. 74). Born 1794; died 1854.

Returning, we continue up Dundas Street to

GREAT KING STREET.

At No. 72 died SIR WILLIAM ALLAN, President of the Royal Scottish Academy of Painting, and for a long period

the only resident historical painter of his country. 'His name,' writes Anderson (*The Scottish Nation*), 'will be always endeared to the admirers of Sir Walter Scott by the strong partiality which the latter evinced on all occasions for his friend 'Willie Allan.' In advanced life, among the literary circles of Edinburgh, Allan was fond of telling how, when a lad of thirteen, employed in painting certain anatomical preparations at Surgeons' Square Hall, he got 'locked up by mistake at night in the room where he had been occupied all day,

GREAT KING STREET.

and was thus compelled to spend the hours of darkness amidst the skeletons and mangled relics of the dead. The hideous effects upon the imagination of a timid susceptible boy in such a charnel-house; the sights he saw by the glimmer of the moon through the crevices of the window shutters, and the still more terrible phantasms which his fancy conjured up, formed such a night of horror as no artist but Fuseli could have realised.' Allan's travels in search of subjects for his pencil extended over Morocco, Greece, Spain, Russia, and Persia. 'He was not a great painter,' says the writer of the notice of his life in the *Dictionary of National Biography*, 'but he deserves to be remembered in the history of English art for the impulse he gave to historical composition, and the example he set in depicting the manners of unfrequented countries.' He died in 1852, at the age of sixty-eight.

At No. 60 the famous preacher and founder of a sect, the REV. EDWARD IRVING, resided, when visiting Edinburgh to deliver a series of twelve lectures on the Apocalypse in 1828. Mrs. Oliphant, in her *Life of Irving*, says: 'He went to live in the house of Mr. Bridges, now a friend of some years' standing, who lived in Great King Street, one of those doleful lines of handsome houses which weigh down the cheerful hill-side under tons of monotonous stone'; and here he is described as being found by a visitor 'with one of the children of the house playing on the carpet at his feet,' possibly the child who was present at Mrs. Bridges' first introduction to, and reception of him, and his kindly notice of whom quickly stilled the nervous apprehensiveness of the mother on encountering the great preacher. Irving was used to children: Carlyle writes of his 'noisy brat' at Myddleton Terrace, Islington, in 1822. It is recorded of Irving's marvellous powers of voice that when preaching at Monimail, in Fife, in the open air, his sermon was distinctly heard by a lady seated at a window a quarter of a mile off; while his voice was audible, though not distinctly, at twice that distance. Irving's sermons and prayers were alike of inordinate length, and his London congregation after a time greatly decreased in consequence. Dr. Chalmers opened the Regent Square Chapel, and the place was filled three hours beforehand by people anxious to hear the great Scottish preacher. Irving offered to 'assist' Chalmers by reading a chapter in the first instance. 'He chose,' said Chalmers, 'the longest chapter in the Bible, and gave an exposition of an hour and a half. When my turn came, of what use could I be in an exhausted receiver.' When Irving offered him a similar service on another occasion, adding, 'I can be short'; 'How long will it take you?'

asked Chalmers. 'Only about an hour and forty minutes.'
'"Then," I replied, "I must decline the favour."'
Prayers of an hour and a half, and sermons of two hours
came to be a common experience in the London chapel,
and a proportionate amount of inconvenience was sometimes incurred in private assemblies. Being, on one
occasion, 'invited to a supper party, and requested by
the host before the meal to read the Bible and expound,
he went on till midnight; when, some of the guests having
several miles to walk home, the host gently suggested his
coming to a close. "Who art thou?" he replied, with pro-
phetic energy, "who darest to interrupt the man of God in
his administrations?" He pursued his commentary for some
time longer, then closed the book, and waving his long arm
over the head of his host, uttered an audible and deliberate
prayer that his offence might be forgiven him.' Irving was
born in 1792, and died in 1824.

No. 16 was at two periods the residence of SIR WILLIAM
HAMILTON. He removed hither from Howe Street in 1827,
at his mother's death, which was a source of great grief to
him. 'Mr. de Quincey' we read in Veitch's *Memoir* 'used
to break in on his evening solitude, accompanied generally
by his eldest son and daughter, children of about eight or
ten years of age. While the two philosophers discoursed
till the small hours of the morning, the two children would
be lying asleep on a chair.' On his marriage in 1829 Sir
William removed to Manor Place, but returned to the house
in Great King Street in 1839. The *Memoir* contains an
interesting description of the interior, contributed by 'a
neighbour in King Street.' 'The rooms in which he and his
family usually sat were surrounded by books; how clearly
does one, in which we passed many a pleasant hour, rise to
mind! In it, from floor to roof, the bookshelves mounted, one
above another, almost entirely covering the walls.' Beneath,
'some fine engravings of the Italian poets,' 'on a table inlaid
with brass, stood two handsome malachite vases, some pieces
of old china, and usually a glass with flowers. . . . The room
was lighted by one large window, and in its entrance stood
a great Indian jar covered with strange devices, and which
must have had a charmed life, since it had survived many
generations of children unscathed. Outside the window
the top of a tall poplar (planted in the court below) swayed
to and fro with every breath of air.' Veitch, in his *Memoir*,
quotes Dr. von Scheel, who wrote: 'Every respectable
German who arrives in Edinburgh has a home in his house,

and, even in intellectual respects, he here finds himself at
home.' He says also: 'He is undoubtedly one of the first-
class scholars living in Great Britain. . . . His reading is
immense, for he has considered no branch of science entirely
foreign to his pursuits, and his memory is admirable.' Sir
William was made Professor of Logic and Metaphysics in
1836. During the last twelve years of his life, he was comparatively helpless from the effects of paralysis, but his
brain was unaffected to the last. He died here: the motto
on his tomb so happily characterises the philosopher and
the man, that it is worth quoting it entirely. 'His aim
was by a pure philosophy to teach that now we see through
a glass darkly. Now we know in part. His hope that in
the life to come he should see face to face, and know even
also as he is known' (see HAMILTON, pp. 76, 89). Born in 1788,
he died in 1856.

At the end of Great King Street is

DRUMMOND PLACE.

At No. 28, on the north side, CHARLES KIRKPATRICK
SHARPE was living for some years before his death. He
has been well described as 'a man of fashion, devoting his
leisure hours to the successful cultivation of literature,
music, and the fine arts.' In Chambers's *Biographical
Dictionary* he is described as 'peculiar in personal appearance, and in the style of his dress—which belonged to a
past rather than the present fashion,' which 'claimed for
him an individuality as singular as it might seem eccentric.
His manners had all that gracefulness and ease—familiar,
yet polite—which distinguish the highly aristocratic school
in which he had been brought up.' His works of literary
and antiquarian interest were produced chiefly between
1827 and 1837. Scott, in his *Journal*, 1825, writes of Sharpe,
that he 'is a very complete genealogist, and has made many
detections in *Douglas* and other books on pedigree which
our nobles would do well to suppress if they had an oppor-
tunity. Strange that a man should be so curious after
scandal of a century old. Not but that Charles loves it fresh
and fresh also; for being very much a fashionable man,
he is always master of the reigning report, and he tells
the anecdotes with such gusto that there is no helping
sympathising with him; a peculiar voice adding not a
little to the general effect. My idea is that Charles Kirkpatrick Sharpe, with his oddities, tastes, satire, and high

aristocratic feelings, resembles Horace Walpole, perhaps in his person also in a general way' (Lockhart's *Scott*). Sharpe died in 1851, at the age of seventy-one (see SHARPE, p. 52).

Returning along the west side of Drummond Place, a turning to the right and another to the left brings us to the centre of

ABERCROMBY PLACE.

At No. 21 WILLIAM EDMONDSTOUNE AYTOUN was born in 1813 (see AYTOUN, pp. 81, 106).

No. 2 was the residence of LORD WEBB SEYMOUR after quitting his house at Glenarbach. He writes from here to Hallam in 1814, who says of him: 'Lord Webb Seymour was neither a very good scholar in the common sense of the word, nor by any means the contrary. . . . His peculiar quality was the love of truth. . . . It was said of him that he would rather get at anything by the longest process; and in fact, not have a quick intuition; and well knowing that those who decide instantly are apt not to understand what they decide, he felt a reluctance to acquiesce in what the world calls a common sense view of any philosophical question . . . . Not only was Lord Webb Seymour a man of the most untainted honour and scrupulous integrity, but of the greatest benevolence, and the warmest attachment to his friends.' (Horner's *Memoirs and Correspondence, Appendix*). Hallam also finds a resemblance to Marcus Aurelius, in the absence of any of the violent passions, 'the mild Stoicism of his character, the self-command which never degenerated into selfishness.' He was the associate of Horner, Playfair, Sir James Hall, Dugald Stewart, and Henry Mackenzie. Lord Cockburn, who has a joke at the 'vastness and slowness of his preparations,' in which he says Seymour habitually joined, remarks that 'the long voluntary residence of this stranger among us excited a deeper sympathy with his fate.'—Lord Webb Seymour died after a long decline, in the year 1819.

ALBANY STREET.

No. 10 appears in the Edinburgh Directory for 1818 as in the occupation of JOHN PLAYFAIR, Professor of Natural

Philosophy. Two years before he was, according to the same source of information, at 2 Albany Street, or, as it was called up to that time, Albany Row. His chief residence after his accession to the Chair of Natural Philosophy in 1805 was at Burntisland. The biographical account prefacing his *Works* states that he spent a 'portion of the summer vacation almost every year in travelling through the more interesting districts of England, Scotland and Wales, in the prosecution of his geological studies; and visited France and Switzerland at the age of sixty-eight;' 'by regular exercise and frequent excursions, Mr. Playfair preserved a degree of activity and a power of exertion rarely to be met with in literary men at a much earlier period of life.' Cockburn says that Playfair was 'admired by all men, and beloved by all women, of whose virtues and intellect he was always the champion: society felt itself the happier and more respectable from his presence. "Philandering at the Needles" was a phrase by which Jeffrey denoted his devotedness to ladies and to books. . . . . Profound yet cheerful; social, yet always respectable, strong in his feelings, but uniformly gentle; a universal favourite, yet never moved from his simplicity; in humble circumstances, but contented and charitable—he realised our idea of an amiable philosopher . . . . I have been told that, when racked on his death-bed with pain, a relation wished to amuse him by reading one of Scott's novels, but that he said he would rather try the *Principia*'

10 ALBANY STREET.

(*Memorials of My Time*). R. P. Gillies, in his *Reminiscences*, says of him that he 'went into society without reluctance, for it seemed as if his tone of nerves and quiet good-humour were so equable and perfectly imperturbable, that nothing discomposed him or "put him out of the way."' He gives an account of a 'convivial meeting' where Playfair was mercilessly bantered for a remark that, in his opinion, 'it might be quite practicable to illuminate the whole of Edinburgh or any other large town, with artificial light by means of inflammable air alone'—an idea carried into practice five years later, and of which some experiments had already been reported, in the introduction of gas. ' "That'll no be till the deevil gangs blind, I'm thinking," interposed the ultra-sagacious Mr. John Clerk . . . . "Professor, can you guarantee us against accidents? if your pipes should happen to leak, the whole house would be charged with hydrogen." "On such premises, of course I could not give any guarantee," replied Mr. Playfair; "very serious accidents might be apprehended." . . . . " I wad pit up with the licht o' an *oilie crusie* rather than venture the gauze into my premises," replied Mr. Clerk.' Playfair died in 1819, at the age of seventy-one. Mr. James Grant, in *Old and New Edinburgh*, says that he died at No. 2. The change of residence indicated by the directories of the period seems to have escaped his notice.

At No. **18** JAMES BALLANTYNE was living from about 1830. In April 1829 Scott writes in his diary : ' I had news of James Ballantyne, hypochondriac, I am afraid, and religiously distressed in mind.' He died in 1833, at the age of sixty-one (see BALLANTYNE, p. 17, 91).

At No. **38** lived SUSAN EDMONSTON FERRIER, author of *Destiny, Marriage* and *The Inheritance*, in the house of her brother, Walter Ferrier. The first of her novels, for which Blackwood paid her £150, was written in 1818, at the time when she kept house for her widowed father, who died in 1829. 'She led a quiet life,' we read in the *Dictionary of National Biography*, 'between Morningside House and Edinburgh, with occasional visits to her sisters. A description by herself of these visits appeared in the *Temple Bar Magazine* for February 1874, and is reprinted in her works. Brougham is said to have been 'an old school-fellow,' and received her courteously when he made a tour of Scotland as Lord Chancellor in 1834. Among other admirers were Joanna Baillie, Sydney Smith, Macaulay, and Sir James Mackintosh. In his *Journal* Scott calls her 'simple, full of humour, and exceedingly ready at repartee, and all this without the least affectation of the blue-stocking.' . . . . Her eye-sight failed, and she had to pass most of her time in a darkened room, receiving a few friends at tea in the evening, but leading a very retired life. The popularity of her first novel was so great that for the second, *The Inheritance*, she received from Blackwood the sum of £1000. She died here in 1854, at the age of seventy.

At No. **51** DR. JOHN BROWN, the author of *Horæ Subsecivæ* and *Rab and his Friends* was living in 1846 (see BROWN, p. 73).

Passing to the left in Union Street, at the end of Forth
Street, a turning to the right leads to

GAYFIELD SQUARE.

No. 10, in a short street at the nearest or north-west
corner, was the residence of the eminent expositor of theology
and preacher, DR. JOHN BROWN, who succeeded Dr. James
Hall in 1822 at Rose Street Chapel, and at whose services it is
said the crowd was so dense at times, that he was led from the
session-house to the pulpit hand to hand across the pews. In
Anderson's *Scottish Nation* we read: 'His personal appearance, which was fine and dignified, was previously to his
death, greatly changed, [owing to ill-health] in reference to
which he himself expressively said, 'The Master changes our
countenance and "sends us away."' He was twice married,
and his second wife predeceased him by seventeen years. Dr.
Brown's popularity was due to the excellent material of
which his sermons were composed, and had nothing in
common with that of the 'fashionable preacher.' Dr.
Brown appears to have had a way, unconsciously, of
fixing individuals in his congregation with his eye in
a manner which sometimes had embarrassing results.
'On one occasion,' writes Dr. Cairns in his *Life* of Brown,
'a woman called on him on a Monday in a state of high
displeasure, to complain that on the foregoing day he had
publicly called her "hypocrite." Dr. Brown disclaimed
all such personality; but the woman warmly rejoined, "You
need not deny it, sir; for you looked straight in my face
when you said it."' Dr Brown died at Arthur Lodge, Newington, in 1858, at the age of seventy-four.

WINDSOR STREET

is in the rear of Elm Row, on the east side of Leith Walk.
    At No. 23 lived about 1835-1850, WILLIAM MURRAY, who
retired into private life in the latter year after a career of
forty years as actor and manager in Edinburgh. At first the
public would have none of him as an actor, but by persis-
tent study he achieved a high professional position; and as
manager was much esteemed and respected. Beyond a brief
record of his career, prefixed to a collection of his speeches

at the close of the several seasons of his theatre, his life does not appear to have afforded material of a biographical character.

About a quarter of a mile distant, reached by turning down Pilrig Street out of Leith Walk, on the left, going northward, lies

SPEY STREET,

a street of old houses, formerly called Moray Street. Here, at No. 2, THOMAS CARLYLE lived 1822-24. He had been in

Edinburgh, with intervals of absence, since walking the hundred miles from Ecclefechan, in company with 'Palinurus Tom,' at the age of fourteen, in 1809, when he lodged in Simon Square. Ten years later, already a dyspeptic, he finds living, in a lodging unrecorded, 'very high. An hour ago I paid my week's bill, which, though 15s. 2d., was the smallest of the three I have yet discharged. This is an unreasonable sum when I consider the slender accommodation, and the paltry ill-cooked morsel which is my daily pittance.' When living in Moray Street, writes Mr. Froude, whose work is the source of our information, 'Carlyle was at ease in his circumstances. He could help his brother : he had no more money anxieties.' A letter from here to his mother dated June 2d, 1822, contains a graphic account of sleepless nights, due to a howling dog in the vicinity, 'an ugly *messan* which a half-crazy half-pay captain thought proper to chain in his garden,' about twenty yards from Carlyle's window, against which complaints proved fruitless. One night, 'I listened about half-an-hour, then rose indignantly, put on my clothes, went out, and charged the watchman to put a stop to the accursed thing. The watchman *would* not for the world interfere with a gentleman's rest at that hour, but next morning he would certainly, etc. I asked to be shown the door, and pulling the crazy captain's bell about six times, his servant at length awoke, and inquired in a tremulous voice *What was it ?* I alluded to the

2 SPEY STREET.

dog and demanded the instant, the total, the everlasting
removal of it, or to-morrow I would see whether justice was
in Edinburgh or the shadow of British law in force. ' Do
you hear that?" said the Irish knight of the rattle and the
lanthorn. She heard it and obeyed, and no wretched *messan*
has since disturbed my slumbers.' At this time, Carlyle
was receiving fifteen guineas a sheet for his *Life of Schiller*,
as well as teaching. Carlyle was born 1795 ; died 1881 (see
CARLYLE, pp. 85, 100, 103).

SUBURBAN ROUTES.

NORTH-WEST SUBURB.

CROSSING the Dean Bridge, Clarendon Crescent and Learmonth Terrace to the *right,* lead to

ANN STREET.

No. 29 was for several years the residence of JOHN WILSON before his removal to Gloucester Place. His daughter and biographer, Mrs. Gordon, writes : 'Towards the end of the winter of 1819, my father, with his wife and children, five in number, left his mother's house, 53 Queen Street, and set up his household gods in a rural and somewhat inconvenient house in Ann Street.' Ann Street was

29 ANN STREET.

then quite 'out of town' (see WILSON, pp. 64, 87).

DANUBE STREET

lies north of Ann Street. At No. 7 HORATIO MACCULLOCH resided and produced some of his best pictures (see MACCULLOCH, p. 108).

Danube Street leads directly into

ST. BERNARD'S CRESCENT.

No. 29 was in 1854 the residence of the talented miscellaneous writer, author of one good novel, *Wearyfoot Common,* and editor for several years of Chambers's *Edin-*

burgh Journal, LEITCH RITCHIE. Mr. James Payn in *Some Literary Recollections*, says of him: 'He was one of the last survivors of a set of literary men now almost, if not quite, extinct; it had the culture of the silver-fork school without their affectation, and the simplicity of the Bohemians without their disreputableness. The author of *Wearyfoot Common* had been one of the hardest workers of his time; "As a young husband," he told me, "I have often written for the press for hours, while at the same time my foot has rocked the cradle of a child." . . . In his time Leitch Ritchie had written upon almost every subject under heaven. . . . If he wanted to write upon a particular subject he would contrive to know more about it in twenty-four hours than any man of general information could possibly know. He was, as is well-known, the companion of Turner in his continental travels, and an authority on matters of art; and he once wrote a pamphlet for an aurist, which made that gentleman's professional reputation.' Ritchie died in London, aged sixty-four, in the year 1865.

Passing the Schoolhouse at the western extremity of St. Bernard's Crescent, we turn up the half-built Dean Park Street, and turning to the right at the end reach, on the south side of the road,

MARY PLACE.

At No. **5**, at one period of his career lived the 'poet-painter' DAVID SCOTT (see SCOTT, p. 45).

Returning westward on the main road, we reach

COMELY BANK.

No. **5** was at one time the residence of JOHN EWBANK (see EWBANK, p. 89).

21 COMELY BANK.

No. **21** was the residence for eighteen months following his marriage, 1826-8, of THOMAS CARLYLE. In May 1826, he writes: 'House in Comely Bank suitable as possible has been chosen; was being furnished from Haddington, beautifully, perfectly, and even richly, by Mrs. Welsh's great skill in such matters, aided by her daughter's, which was also great, and by the frank *wordless* generosity of both, which surely was very great.' 'Mrs. Welsh undertook to pay the rent,' writes Mr. Froude, 'and the Haddington furniture was carried thither. She proposed to remain there with her daughter till October, and was then to remove finally to her father's. . . . For immediate expenses of living there was Carlyle's £200, and such additions to it as he could earn.' This was little enough, a novel was written, found no publisher, and was burned. His reputation was yet to make. Miss Welsh writes from Comely Bank to her affianced, describing the house : 'It would be quite country-looking, only that it is one of a range ; for there is a real flower-garden in front, overshadowed by a far-spreading tree, while the windows look out on the greenest fields, with never a street to be seen. As for interior accommodation, there are a dining-room, three sleeping-rooms, a kitchen, and more closets than I can see the least occasion for; unless you design to be another Blue Beard. So you see we shall have apartments enough, on a small scale, indeed, almost laughably small; but this is no objection in your eyes, neither is it in mine.' Notwithstanding Carlyle's expressed intention to 'treat visitors as nauseous intruders,' Mrs. Carlyle had her tea-parties, 'and no one who had been once at Comely Bank refused a second invitation. Brewster came, and De Quincey . . . and Sir William Hamilton, and Wilson, (though Wilson, for some reason, was shy of Carlyle), and many more.' Carlyle's own picture of his life here is given in a letter to Alexander Carlyle, on February 3d, 1827 : 'Directly after breakfast, the good wife and the Doctor [his brother John, who was staying with them] retire upstairs to the drawing-room, a little place all fitted up like a lady's work-box, where a spunk of fire is lit for the forenoon ; and I meanwhile sit scribbling and meditating, and wrestling with the powers of dulness till one or two o'clock ; when I sally forth into the city or towards the sea-shore, taking care only to be home for the important purpose of consuming my mutton chop at four. After dinner we all read learned languages till coffee (which we now often take at night instead of tea), and so on till bed-time ; only that Jane often sews ; and the Doctor goes up to the celestial globe, studying the fixed stars through an upshoved window, and generally comes down to his porridge about ten, with a nose dripping at its extremity. Thus we pass our days in our little cottage. . . . Many a time, on a soft mild night, I smoke my pipe in our little flower garden, and look upon all this, and think of all absent and present friends, and feel that I have good reason "to be thankful I am not in Purgatory."' In the spring of 1828 they went to Craigenputtock, where, before marriage, Mrs. Carlyle had told him 'she could not live a month with an angel,' and shortly afterwards to London. Carlyle died in 1881, aged 86 (see CARLYLE, p. 85).

CRAIGLEITH,

a station on the Caledonian Railway, two miles from the city, is within about a mile of

CRAIGCROOK CASTLE,

the most ancient part of which dates from the middle of the sixteenth century. ARCHIBALD CONSTABLE occupied and greatly improved the house in the early years of the present century, and here his son and biographer, THOMAS CONSTABLE, was born in 1812. He began business, writes Grant (*Old and New Edinburgh*) in 1833, 'and by his taste and care did more than any other man, perhaps, to raise the printing trade in Edinburgh to the high position it now holds.' He died in 1881 (see CONSTABLE, p. 46).

Craigcrook was from the year 1815 the summer residence of FRANCIS JEFFREY. Cockburn, in his *Journal* (1846), calls it 'The Paradise of Edinburgh Villas.' 'In 1816,' he says, 'the house was not unlike its neighbour Lauriston—a keep, though not so bare. It then became the residence of Jeffrey, who, aided by Playfair, has made it what it is.

CRAIGCROOK.

Nothing could be more perfect. It has been enlarged truly in the old spirit. The domestic scenery of the outside is Jeffrey's own creation. He has had the sense to venerate

old walls and gorgeous ivy, and to resist doing or keeping
more than can easily be done and kept well: so old, yet so
comfortable; so picturesque and so sensible; so beautifully
small within the garden, but with such rich soft over-turf
outside.   What a wood-grown hill; the absence of prospects from the low ground compensated by such views,
unrivalled even for Edinburgh, from the higher.   These will
ever be its charms to strangers; but to us it is Jeffrey that
we see in Craigcrook.   It is here that for thirty years he has
enjoyed and diffused the finest pleasures of the head and of
the heart. . . . Who that has known the place in his time
can ever think of it without hearing that sweet and lively
voice, without feeling admiration of his genius, lost under
the inspiration of his goodness' (see JEFFREY, pp. 32, 42, 55,
63, 84).

About a mile westward from Craigcrook is

LAURISTON CASTLE,

in the beginning of the last century the property of the
famous financier JOHN LAW, who inherited it from his
father, a wealthy goldsmith of Edinburgh, and who is said
to have been born in the tower in 1671.   The additions to the
old square three-storied tower were made by Mr. Burn the
architect for the late Lord Rutherfurd.

NORTHERN SUBURB.

INVERLEITH TERRACE.

The house formerly standing on the site of the present
No. 1 was the residence from 1849 to 1853 of WILLIAM
EDMONDSTOUNE AYTOUN, and a far from comfortable one,
as appears from a letter in the Life by Sir Theodore Martin :
'The house we occupy at present is a very small one and
very ill-furnished.   This winter the rains have been so violent that they have absolutely penetrated the outer wall
(ours is a corner house), and the upper story is uninhabitable.'
He came here on his marriage, and subsequently removed to a
house in Great Stuart Street.   Writing of him as he was in
1843, his biographer says : ' A more delightful companion than
Aytoun was at this period it would be difficult to imagine.
Full of health and vigour, and with a flow of spirits which
seemed inexhaustible, his society acted like a tonic on men of
a more sensitive temperament and a constitution less robust.

There was a charm of humour about his talk which it would be hard to define. It was compounded mainly of pleasant exaggeration, playful allusion, unlooked-for turns of phrase, and strong mother-wit. It was always essentially the humour of a gentleman, without cynicism and without irreverence.' As is well-known, Aytoun had the credit of editing *Blackwood's Magazine* after Professor Wilson's, his father-in-law's, death. As a matter of fact, Blackwood was his own editor. Aytoun was a contributor to the *Magazine* from 1839, and his *Lays of the Scottish Cavaliers* first appeared in its pages. He was born in 1813, and died 1865 (see AYTOUN, pp. 81, 96).

INVERLEITH ROW.

No. 7 was for some years previous to 1843—when he removed to Morningside—the residence of the REV. DR. CHAL-MERS. Lord Cockburn (*Memorials of My Time*) says of him : 'There can scarcely be a more curious man. When I first became acquainted with him, he used to leave his parish of Kilmany [in Fife] twice or thrice a week to lecture in St. Andrews on chemistry. And not confining himself to physical science, he stored his mind during this first stage of his course by a general study of the principles of moral and political philosophy. . . . But it was only on being elevated by the deep religious feelings which afterwards took possession of him that his powers were developed in their full force. . . . He is awkward, and has a low husky voice, a guttural articulation, a whitish eye, and a large dingy countenance. In point of mere feature it would not be difficult to think him ugly. But he is saved from this, and made interesting and lovable by singular modesty, kindness, and simplicity of manner, a strong expression of calm thought and benevolence, a forehead so broad that it seems to proclaim itself the seat of a great intellect, a love of humour, and an indescribable look of drollery when anything ludicrous comes over him.' In Hanna's *Memoirs of Chalmers* we are told that 'his invariable mode of dealing with introductions was to invite the introduced to breakfast ; very interesting groups often gathered round his breakfast-table. In the general conversation of promiscuous society, Dr. Chalmers did not excel.' In Anderson's *Scottish Nation* we read : 'His accent and appearance were both against him. The former was broad provincial Scotch, the latter was dull and heavy, and by no means conveyed any idea of the wonderful fertility and energy of his mind. In stature he was about the middle height, stout, large-boned, and muscular, but not at all approaching to corpulency. His grey eye, which in his ordinary mood had a placid expression, when excited shone with intense brilliancy; his forehead was broad and massy, but not particularly lofty, his step was quick and eager, his gesture awkward, and his delivery monotonous; but yet, when roused from his lethargy, when fairly within his subject, these drawbacks were all forgotten in the rapid stream of his eloquence.' And so it came about that when he first preached in London, and his celebrity filled Surrey Chapel four hours before the service commenced, Canning, who was among his hearers, was heard to say after one of the preacher's true bursts of oratory, 'This is indeed true eloquence. The tartan beats us all.' Chalmers, it is said, did almost everything by numbers. His razor received one additional stroke on the strop each day up to a certain number; then daily one less. His stick was put down at each fourth footfall, and he mechanically counted the number of descents to measure the distance. He would go round his garden, and returning, say, 'Well, dearie daughts, it's a noble instrument a garden. I've just counted all the things in flower round all the walks, and they are 320.' He was entirely indifferent about food, and remarkably abstemious, and actually entered in his journal on one occasion, 'Exceeded to-night at supper,' when all he had consumed was a large water-biscuit as thin as a wafer. He imposed on himself the problem of discover ing each day a new route through the complication of streets that lay between him and the University, and keeping a record of their relative lengths. Next to the pleasure of being introduced to a new locality was that of thoroughly exploring one already known. 'I like,' he said to one of his students, 'to find out new spots in places I am familiar with. The other day I had some time to spare, so I tried if I could extemporise a new route between Comely Bank and Inverleith Row. I sauntered, rather dubious, I must confess, up a sort of cart-lane, and, before I was aware, I got involved in the accessories of a farm-house, where I was set upon by a mastiff and obliged to turn back.' Dr. Chalmers died in 1847, aged sixty-seven (see CHALMERS, pp. 62, 117).

At No. **54**, HORATIO MacCULLOCH, the artist *par excellence* of Scottish landscape, was living in 1850; a man of singular modesty and simplicity, and warmth of heart. 'Although of robust constitution,' says the writer of his Memoir in

Chambers's *Biographical Dictionary*, 'incessant application and out-door exposure to change of weather began to tell upon his frame, and about fifteen years before his death, after having sat working in the open air at Smallholme, he was attacked by a slight shock of paralysis, which affected his left side and the muscles of his face. . . . In the winter of 1866 he experienced a second and still more severe stroke, from which he rallied with similar readiness, and resumed his wonted occupation; but in February of the following year, the third and worst attack, which proved to be the final summons, occurred, and on the 24th June 1867 he expired in the sixty-second year of his age. In 1862 he was living at St. Colm Villa, Trinity (see MacCulloch, p. 102).

EASTERN SUBURBS.

PORTOBELLO

is three miles distant eastward from Edinburgh, and is reached either by railway, or by tramcar from the Post Office.

No. 18½ **High Street,** next to the Church of St. Mark, was formerly known as Shrub Mount, and was the residence of HUGH MILLER in the closing years of his life. The lower part of a portion of the two-story house is turned into a shop; and the former entrance must be sought up a passage to the right. Here are two pillars which formerly faced the garden, and the entrance hall in front of which they stand is now divided; as is the house itself, so as to form two residences. Hugh Miller purchased the house, and added a museum for his geological and other specimens. In 1852 he began to lecture on popular science, and it is said that, he succeeded in imparting to his audience something of his own absorbing and sympathetic interest in his subject. Later on, indications of intellectual disturbance became apparent at times, which were carefully concealed from his doctor until too late, and the evil had become confirmed. A dread of robbery and assassination haunted him on his walks by night from Edinburgh to his house. He had fears also for the safety of the contents of his museum. This led to the acquisition of a revolver, a claymore, and a dagger, and in sleep the weapons lay ready to his hand. Being accustomed to work far into the morning, to avoid disturbing his wife, whose health was delicate, he occupied a room at a distance from the family, and here on the morning of Christmas Day 1856, his lifeless body was found half-dressed upon the floor, and an open letter to his wife upon the table: 'Dearest Lydia,—My brain burns. I *must* have *walked* ; and a fearful dream rises upon me. I cannot bear the horrible thought. God and the Father of the Lord Jesus Christ have mercy upon me. Dearest Lydia, dear children, farewell. My brain burns as the recollection grows. My dear, dear wife, farewell.—Hugh Miller.' It is assumed that he was attacked by one of the horrible trances that had proved too strong for him. He had shot himself through the lung with the weapon which lay in such unfortunate proximity to his hand. Many interesting particulars of Hugh Miller are given from personal knowledge in Anderson's *Scottish Nation.* 'His habits of composition,' says the writer, 'were peculiar. His mind, with all its weight and force, and in spite of the rich intellectual stores which he possessed, wanted elasticity ; and he was in general, a slow and cautious writer. Before putting pen to paper on any subject, he spent a long time in deep thought, arranging, as it were, all its details within himself ; meanwhile balancing the poker or the tongs in his hand or gazing musingly into the fire. . . . He was fond of athletic exercises, and took delight in such acts as leaping on the table, poising a chair by one of its hind legs in his right hand, and doing other feats of strength in which no one present could compete with him. He also took a pride in snuffing a candle by the mere wave of his arm, when no other arm, though half a yard nearer, could do it.' Miller was fifty-four years of age at the time of his death (see MILLER, p. 44).

SOUTH-EAST SUBURB.

A Newington car takes us from the General Post-office to

SOUTH BLACKET PLACE.

Newington House was the residence from 1860 until his death, a quarter of a century later, of DUNCAN M'LAREN. In a notice of his recently published *Life*, *The Times* of September 12th 1889, says: 'Beginning as a shop-boy he became one of the foremost citizens in a city that used to be governed by men of the robe, and prided itself on its aristocratic prejudices. And having made his way by breaching and levelling the barriers which opposed his progress, he obtained the esteem of his opponents, whose interests he had injured. They might not like his manners or his methods, but they did justice to his motives and his public spirit. In many respects he resembled his distinguished brother-in-law, John Bright.' In his youth 'he read everything that came within his reach. He seems to have grounded himself chiefly on two great volumes of an encyclopædia, and he is said to have swallowed all the contents, except algebra and mathematics, which he found indigestible.' As he became more engrossed with public affairs, M'Laren withdrew gradually from the flourishing business which still bears his name. He died in 1886, aged eighty-six.

At the end of Blacket Place, the Dalkeith Road leads, on the left, to

SALISBURY ROAD.

No. 1 was the last residence in Edinburgh of DR. THOMAS GUTHRIE. In his *Autobiography*, referring complacently to his economy in the matter of rent, he says he paid only £40 a year for his house in Lauriston Lane, 'a rent which rose to no more than £42 before I stepped from being a tenant of that low-rented, old-fashioned, plain abode, to become owner and occupant of 1 Salisbury Road; whence I have a view of Arthur's Seat, Salisbury Crags, and the remarkable crystallised trap rock called Samson's Ribs, of Duddingston Loch, with its wooded banks, swans, and picturesque church; and of the sea beyond, breaking on

1 SALISBURY ROAD.

the shores of Aberlady Bay—a scene of the most beautiful description spread out before me in its glory of a fine summer morning without lifting my head from the pillow.' He died 1873, at the age of seventy (see GUTHRIE, p. 43).

No. 2, from about 1815 to 1830, was the residence of WILLIAM BLACKWOOD. His famous *Magazine* was com-

menced in 1817. In a number of the year 1834 appeared
an obituary notice from which we extract the following:
'No man ever conducted business in a more direct and manly
manner than Mr. Blackwood. His opinion was on all
occasions distinctly explained; his questions were ever
explicit; his answers conclusive. His sincerity might sometimes be considered as rough, but no human being ever
accused him of either flattering or of shuffling; and those
men of letters who were in frequent communication with
him soon conceived a respect and confidence for him, which,
save in a very few instances, ripened into cordial regard
and friendship.' In *Peter's Letters to his Kinsfolk*, Lockhart
describes him as 'nimble, active-looking, with a complexion
very sanguineous; . . nothing can be more sagacious than
the expression of his whole physiognomy—the grey eyes
and eyebrows full of locomotion.' William Blackwood was
born 1776; died 1834 (see BLACKWOOD, pp. 47, 54, 84).

Passing through Salisbury Place at the end of Salisbury
Road, and turning northward up Causewayside, we reach on
the left,

BRAID PLACE

No. 7 was formerly the rear of Sciennes Hill House,
by generally accepted tradition the residence of DR. ADAM
FERGUSON, the historian. It stood alone, enclosed within
walls, with a gate where Gibbs' dairy now stands in Sciennes
Gardens, the entrance being on the first floor, by an outside
stair. The place where the doorway was walled up may
be seen from the court in the rear of No. 7, formerly the
garden. Here Scott and Burns met for the first and last
time. Scott writing of 1786-7, says: 'I saw him one day
at the late venerable Professor Ferguson's, where there
were several gentlemen of literary reputation, among whom
I remember the celebrated Mr. Dugald Stewart. Of course
we youngsters sat silent, and looked and listened.' It is
worthy of note that this region was then considered
so remote that Cockburn's friends called it *Kamtschatka*.
Ferguson is described as active, muscular and well formed,
with fair complexion, blue eyes, and handsome, thoughtful,
intelligent features. Lord Cockburn's recollection of him
in old age is with 'hair silky white, eyes animated and
bright blue; his cheeks sprinkled with broken red, like
autumnal apples, but fresh and healthy. . . . A severe
paralytic attack had reduced his animal vitality though it
left no external appearance, and he required considerable

artificial heat. His raiment, therefore, consisted of half
boots, lined with fur, cloth breeches, a long cloth waistcoat,
with capacious pockets, a single-breasted coat, a cloth
great coat, also lined with fur, and a felt hat commonly
tied by a ribbon below the chin. . . . His gait and air were
noble, his gestures slow; his look full of dignity and
composed fire. He looked like a philosopher from Lapland.'
He is said to have kept the paralytic symptoms in check by
a vegetable diet. Cockburn says: 'Wine and animal food
besought his appetite in vain, but huge masses of milk and
vegetables disappeared before him.' From the same source
we learn that 'his temperature was regulated by Fahren-
heit, and often, when sitting quite comfortably, he would
start up and put his wife and daughters into commotion,
because his eye had fallen on the instrument, and that he
was a degree too hot or too cold.' His *Roman History* was
produced in 1783, and ten years later, Cockburn says, 'he
shook hands with us boys one day in the summer of 1793,
on setting off, in a strange sort of carriage, and with no
companion except his servant James, to visit Italy, for a
new edition of his *History*. He was then about seventy-two,
and had to pass through a good deal of war; but returned
in about a year, younger than ever.' He retired to St.
Andrews on his return, and lived to be ninety-two, dying
in 1816.

The first point of interest in the next division is at a
distance of two-thirds of a mile from Sciennes.

SOUTH AND SOUTH-WEST SUBURBS.

GRANGE LOAN

turns off to the westward from the southern end of Causewayside. On the right, a little way past Lauder Road, standing
back from the road, from which it is hidden by a seven-foot
wall—at the further end of which a partial view of the house
may be obtained—is

Grange House, now a ladies' school. Here died the REV.
WILLIAM ROBERTSON, D.D., and Principal of the University
of Edinburgh from 1761. This was two years after the
publication of his *History of Scotland*, and his first arrival in
Edinburgh. 'Principal Robertson,' writes Lord Cockburn,

'and his family were very intimate with the family of my father. The Principal dined at our house very often, and

lived for the last two years of his life very near us, in the house of Grange, where he died . . . . He was a very pleasant-looking old man; with an eye of great vivacity and intelligence, a large projecting chin, a small hearing-trumpet fastened by a black ribbon to a button-hole in his coat, and a rather large wig powdered and curled. He struck us boys, even from the side-table, as being evidently fond of a good dinner; at which he sat, with his chin near his plate intent

GRANGE HOUSE.

upon the real business of the occasion. This appearance, however, must have been produced by his deafness, because, when his eye told him there was something interesting, it was delightful to observe the animation with which he instantly applied his trumpet, when, having caught the scent, he followed it up, and was the leader of the pack' (*Memorials of My Time*). 'His whole life was spent in study,' says Lord Brougham (*Life*): 'I well remember his constant habit of quitting the drawing-room both after dinner and after tea; and remaining shut up in his library.' His labours were very profitable. For the copyright of his *History of the Reign of Charles V.* he received £4,500, in 1779—the largest sum then known to have been paid for a single work. The *History of America* appeared the previous year. His colleague, Dr. Erskine, in a sermon preached after his death said: 'Few minds were naturally so large and capacious as Dr. Robertson's, or stored by study, experience, and observation with so rich furniture. His imagination was correct, his judgment sound, his memory tenacious, his temper agreeable, his knowledge extensive, and his acquaintance with the world and with the heart of man very remarkable.' Robertson is described as rather above the middle size, and his form suggested a vigorous and healthy constitution, though deficient in activity. His health began to fail in 1791, and it was then that he removed to Grange House for the advantage of a quiet situation and better air.   His constitution was gradually undermined by jaundice, and he died after a lingering illness in 1793, aged seventy-two (see post).

Grange House was also the residence (1832-1848), of SIR THOMAS DICK LAUDER, whose multifarious writings included geology, Scottish antiquities, historical romances, and directions for deep-sea fishing: 'an eminently liberal man, who often obeyed the impulses of humanity without due reference to maxims of political economy, or perhaps to the dictates of common prudence.   I well remember, on more than one occasion after breakfasting at Grange House, that home of love and happiness, when leaving it along with him to return to town, the *tribe* of suitors—chiefly female—that beset him in the Lover's Lane, and to each of them he seemed to give a daily and expected dole, from the heavy pocket which he was not long in lightening.   On my venturing to remonstrate, he said: "I only give them pence; if they walk so far for so small a sum they must be needy" (*Archibald Constable and his Literary Correspondents*).   It is said of him in Chambers's *Biographical Dictionary* that 'he was an industrious, public-spirited man, fully conscious of the duties of his position, and indefatigable in promoting the best interests of his country.'   Lord Cockburn, in his *Memorials*, gives a vivid portrait of Sir Thomas Dick Lauder: 'A flow of rambling natural talk; ready jokes, the twinkle of a mild, laughing eye; a profusion of grey grizzly hair tossed over head, face, and throat; a bludgeon ludicrously huge for civil life, especially in his powerful though gentle hand; raiment half fashionable, half agrestic; a tall gentlemanlike, Quixote figure, and a general picturesqueness of appearance . . . He is honourable, warm-hearted, and friendly, overflowing with equity and kindness.'   His death, caused by a tumour in the spine, took place in 1848.   He was fifty-four years of age.

Grange Loan leads at its termination into

WHITE   HOUSE   LOAN.

At the south-west corner of Hope Terrace is THE WHITE HOUSE.   Here DR. WILLIAM ROBERTSON is reported to have written his *History of the Reign of Charles V.*, and, according to a statement in the *Edinburgh Weekly Journal* of April 1820, 'on the authority of a very near relation of Dr. Blair, to whom these particulars were often related by the Doctor with great interest,' JOHN HOME resided here when writing his tragedy of *Douglas*, and HUGH BLAIR himself at the time of the production of his *Lectures*.   Of Home, the only one of these three celebrities not noticed in former sections of this work, and who finally settled in Edinburgh (living at one time in Hanover Street) in 1779, at the age of fifty-six, it is said that he availed himself of an ample income to 'entertain on so large a scale, that he often had his house filled to a degree which would now be considered intolerable with permanent guests.'   As an instance of his extreme carelessness in business matters, it is related that when Dr. Ferguson repaid him £200 which Home had lent him on his note of hand, he wrote that 'to talk of finding any such note among his papers was like talking of finding the lost books of Livy'; and sent in place of it a letter, 'If ever the note appears, it will be no use except to show what a foolish, thoughtless, inattentive fellow I am.'   Dr. Alexander Carlyle, in his *Autobiography*, says of him : 'Home was an admirable companion, ... He was very handsome, and had a fine person, about five feet ten and a half inches—and an agreeable catching address ; he had not much wit, and still less humour, but he had so much sprightliness and vivacity and such an expression of benevolence in his manner, and such an unceasing flattery of those he liked . . . . that he was truly irresistible, and his entry into a company was like opening a window and letting the sun into the room.'   When Home took his play to London to show it to Garrick—who declined it as totally unfit for the stage—he travelled on horseback, and wished to carry the MS. in his pocket, but his friends, trembling for the safety of the drama, their admiration of which he describes as little short of idolatry, procured for him the loan of a couple of saddle-bags.   Its production in Edinburgh, amidst the greatest excitement, as the first production there of an original work by a Scotsman, not only forced him to abdicate his own clerical functions, but got his ministerial friends who attended the performance into trouble with the narrow-minded Presbytery of the time ; one reverend gentleman being 'suspended for a month, as a mitigated sentence in consideration of his apology for conduct into which he had been unwarily led—that he attended the representation only *once*, and endeavoured to conceal himself in a corner, *to avoid giving offence*' (*Life of Home* by H. Mackenzie). Home died in 1808, at the age of eighty-six.

Clinton Road, nearly opposite Hope Terrace, leads to

CHURCH HILL.

At No. 1, in a house which he had built, the REV. DR.
CHALMERS closed his earthly career.   The housekeeper,
going to his room early,
with a message, found him
'half erect, his head rest-
ing gently on the pillow,
the expression of his countenance that of fixed and
majestic repose.' He had
been dead for hours, and
'it must have been wholly
without pain or conflict.'
Writing of his life here,
his biographer, Dr. Hanna,
says: 'Whatever variety
the day exhibited, it had
one fixed essential feature.
. . . The period allotted to
what he called severe "com-

1 CHURCH HILL.

position" never exceeded (if we except his first winter at St.
Andrews) two or three hours at a time ; and in ordinary circumstances there was seldom more than one sitting daily at
such work.   The tension of the mind during the effort was
extreme ; but it was never so long continued as to induce
fatigue or exhaustion.   During the last six or seven years of
his life his daily modicum of composition was completed
before breakfast, written in shorthand, and all done in bed.
The preparatory ruminating and excogitating process was
slow, but it was complete.' Dr. Chalmers removed here from
Inverleith Row in 1843, and 'as the distance was too great
for him to walk from College, he generally drove to the
outskirts of the town.' An additional illustration to those
given in noting his former residence, of his 'doing everything by numbers' is seen in the following extract: 'Whilst
walking from Wright's Houses, the point at which he was
set down, to his house at Church Hill, he one winter kept an
accurate reckoning of the number of persons he met upon
the road each day—curious to know whether a fixed average
would be observed or whether it would vary as the days
shortened or lengthened.' 'He had one morning in the
week,' writes Dr. Hanna, referring to his custom of entertaining at breakfast, 'reserved especially for his students.

On meeting with them in his own house, he was often at a loss to recognise them by name ; and the course he took to extricate himself from the difficulty was rather singular. He had a card with the names on it of all the students whom he had that morning invited to breakfast. When all had assembled and were seated, holding the card below the level of the table, as he thought out of sight, he glanced furtively down at it, to catch the first name on the list. Then, lifting his eyes, and looking eagerly and rapidly around, he would say—"Tea or coffee, Mr. Johnstone?" hoping by this innocent artifice to identify the person so addressed, and to save him the pain of being apparently unknown or forgotten. The device was too transparent to be unnoticed : but who of his students did not love him all the more for the kindliness which dictated it?' Chalmers was born in 1780, and died in 1847, in his sixty-eighth year (see CHALMERS, pp. 62, 107).

INDEX OF RESIDENTS

INDEX OF STREETS, Etc.

Printed by T. and A. CONSTABLE, Printers to Her Majesty,
at the Edinburgh University Press.